WRITING IN RESTAURANTS

WRITING IN
RESTAURANTS

∎

DAVID MAMET

VIKING

VIKING
Viking Penguin Inc., 40 West 23rd Street,
New York, New York 10010, U.S.A.
Penguin Books Ltd, Harmondsworth,
Middlesex, England
Penguin Books Australia Ltd, Ringwood,
Victoria, Australia
Penguin Books Canada Limited, 2801 John Street,
Markham, Ontario, Canada L3R 1B4
Penguin Books (N.Z.) Ltd, 182–190 Wairau Road,
Auckland 10, New Zealand

First published in 1986 by Viking Penguin Inc.
Published simultaneously in Canada

"A National Dream-Life" and "Against Amplification" first appeared in *The Dramatists Guild Quarterly*; "Radio Drama," "Chicago," a portion of "A Playwright in Hollywood," and "Address to the American Theater Critics Convention" in *Horizon*; "First Principles" in *Theatre* (Yale School of Drama); "True Stories of Bitches" in *Vanity Fair*; "A Family Vacation" in *Vogue*; "Oscars" in *Gentlemen's Quarterly*; "Pool Halls" (under the title "American Icons") and "Epitaph for Tennessee Williams" in *Rolling Stone*; a portion of "Things I Have Learned Playing Poker on the Hill" in *The New York Times Magazine*; "Concerning *The Water Engine*" in *The New York Daily News*; and "Realism" in *New York Arts Journal*.

Notes for a Catalogue for Raymond Saunders was published by the Stephen Wirtz Gallery, San Francisco.

LIBRARY OF CONGRESS CATALOGING IN PUBLICATION DATA
Mamet, David.
Writing in restaurants.
I. Title.
PS3563.A4345W7   1986   814'.54   85-41105
ISBN 0-670-81140-8

Printed in the United States of America by
R. R. Donnelley & Sons Company, Harrisonburg, Virginia
Set in Bodoni Book
Designed by Ann Gold

TO LINDSAY ANN CROUSE

PREFACE

Some Russian filmmaker, Eisenstein, or Pudovkin, or Evreinov, wrote that the preeminence of the Soviet directors in the late 1920s was due to this: at the beginning of their careers they had no film. The World War and the Revolution stopped imports of film stock, so all the young filmmakers could do was sit about and theorize for five years, which is what they did.

I spent my twentieth year at the Neighborhood Playhouse School of the Theatre in New York. At the Playhouse we were exposed to, drilled in, and inculcated with the idea of a *unified aesthetic of theater;* that is, a theater whose every aspect (design, performance, lighting, rehearsal procedures, dramaturgy) was subordinated to the Idea of the Play. We were taught that the purpose of the play was to bring to the stage, through the medium of the actors, the life of the human soul.

The awesome technical and spiritual problems posed by a dedication to those ideas fascinated me. How, I wondered, can an actor overcome his self-consciousness while performing in front of people he desperately wants to please; how can the director understand a complex play and communicate his understanding to the actors in simple, physically actable directions; how can the playwright devote himself to the through-action of the play without having his dialogue become tendentious?

These essentially Eastern problems fascinated me no end, and I thought about them constantly. I recognized my state, years later, reading Abraham Cahan's *The Imported Bridegroom*. Reading this book I discovered in myself the racial type of the lapsed Talmudist. In theatrical musings I had, for the first time in my life, discovered a task which I adored, and to which dedication was the exact opposite of drudgery.

In this state of happy student I was a brother to the Soviet filmmakers who had the empty cameras—I was being trained as an actor, but it was a task for which I lacked both disposition and (more important) the discipline to which, perhaps, talent might have enticed me.

What was I to do, then, with my love of theory and lack of outlet? I took the usual path: I became a teacher. At the tender age of twenty-two I became a vehement, possessed teacher of acting.

As a practical laboratory for my Mandarin aesthetic interests, I began directing my students in plays, then I began writing plays for them to do, and that is how I came the long way around the barn to playwriting.

The following pieces reflect, I think, a continuing concern, and, more important, a never-flagging fascination with the two ideas I discovered as a student: (1) every aspect of the production should reflect the idea of the play; (2) the purpose of the play is to bring to the stage the life of the soul.

It is possible that I have—both in the pieces regarding the Theater, and in those treating things which are assuredly none of my business—lapsed at times into dogmatism—I hope it's not the case, and don't think it is, but you may. My makeup today is the same as it was eighteen years ago, essentially that of an unsure student who has finally discovered an idea in which he can believe, and who feels unless he clutches and dedicates himelf to that idea, he will be lost.

D.M.
December 18, 1985

ACKNOWLEDGMENTS

I would like to acknowledge several people who encouraged me to write prose, helped teach me to write better, and appreciated my work sufficiently to publish it or to help me get it published: Mr. Andy Potok; Richard Christiansen of the *Chicago Tribune;* Otis Guernsey of the *Dramatists Guild Quarterly;* Wayne Lawson of *Vanity Fair;* Dawn Seferian of Viking Penguin; and my agent, Andrew Wylie.

CONTENTS

CONTENTS

PART I

WRITING IN RESTAURANTS

CAPTURE-THE-FLAG, MONOTHEISM, AND THE TECHNIQUES OF ARBITRATION

In Chicago's traffic court there is a room set aside for silver-suited lawyers. They sit there all day long, smoking and discussing who got caught, and defendants who wish to cop a plea go to the lawyers' room to shop for an attorney.

There the lawyers sit and, casually, anxiously, they watch the door their clients will come through. They look just like kids waiting for the captain to choose them for his team of Kick-the-Can.

We all were lawyers in the schoolyard. We were concerned with property and honor, and correct application of the magical power of words.

In the narration or recapitulation of serious matters our peers were never said to have "said" things, but to have "gone" things; we ten- and twelve-year-olds thereby recognizing a *statement* as an *action*. (He goes, "Get over to your side of the line, or you're out," and I go, "I am on my side of the line—it runs from the bench to the water fountain.")

Our schoolyard code of honor recognized words as magical and powerful unto themselves, and it was every bit as pompous and self-satisfied in the recognition of its magic as is the copyright code or a liquidated damages clause. It was the language of games, the language of an endeavor which is, in its essence, make-believe—the language of American Business:

ME   I'm goin' down the Shoreland for a phos, I don' wan' Gussie comin' with.

TOM   Why not?

ME   We're playin' ball the *schoolyard* . . . ?

TOM   Football, baseball?

ME   *Baseball.*

TOM   Yeah . . .

ME   We lost the ball.

TOM   Whose ball?

ME   *(Pause) Gussie's.*

TOM   Yeah.

ME   So he goes he ain't going home until we're paying him we lost the ball, he's gonna call my ma.

TOM   Where did you lose it?

ME   On the roof. So I go, "Look, you never called it, Gussie."

TOM   He din *call* it?

ME   *No!* That's what I'm *tellin'* you. He goes "I called it." I go, "No, you didn't, Gussie. No. You never called it, no. If you said 'chips' we woulda heard it, and you never called it. No." I ast the other guys, his own team, huh? Maurice goes, "I don't think you called it, Gus." I go, "Look here, your own man, Gussie, huh?" He says that didn' mean a thing. His own man . . .

TOM   Yeah.

ME   I tell him, "I ain't trine a hock the ball off you, Gus; you called '*chips,*' I'd pay for it right now. It's not the money . . ."

TOM   . . . no . . .

ME   " . . . and you know times that *I* have loss my ball, and you ass Mike or anybody." Huh?

TOM   Yeah.

ME "Or we're up in Jackson Park I got my headlight broke. I didn't say a word acause I din' say 'chips.' (*Pause*) And I have to say you never said it, too."

TOM So what he say?

ME He goes I'm trine a cheat him out his ball. I tell him I will go up there and get it Monday. I would *like* to pay him back...

TOM Uh-huh...

ME I'll go up there and *get* it...

TOM Yeah...

ME But when he didn't *call* it, I can't pay him back. He knows this isn't fair.

TOM Yeah.

ME And I *tole* him that this isn't fair. He *called* it, we would all of played a little carefuller.

This is, no doubt, a somewhat romanticized, but, I feel, essentially accurate rendition of one of our schoolyard negotiations circa 1959; and it differs only in the minutest particulars, the diction, and not at all in spirit, from most adult formal and informal contract negotiations.

Thorstein Veblen said that the more that jargon and technical language is involved in an endeavor, the more we may assume that the endeavor is essentially make-believe.

As in Law, Commerce, Warfare. There we were in Vietnam; there we were in Jackson Park.

"Olley Olley Ocean Free" was our South Side Chicago version of the cry which ends a game of tag. I think the phrase frightened us as children.

We knew that an afternoon of kick-the-can or capture-the-flag could only be positively terminated by the adjuration "Olleyolleyoceanfree," but none of us had one idea what the words *themselves* meant. We only knew they had magical power to cast off the restrictions of the game (to loose us from our vows) and let us go to dinner. (The "free" was clearly pertinent, and the "olley" could, by a stretch, be accepted as a rhythmic aid; but what, in the name of God, did the "ocean" mean?)

The Schoolboy Universe was not corrupted by the written word, and was ruled by the powers of sounds: Cheater's Proof, Sucker's Walk, Rubber Balls, and Liquor. Our language had weight and meaning to the extent to which it was rhythmic and pleasant, and its power came from a juxtaposition of sounds in a world in which we were overtly pantheists.

"American Eagle" was the binding incantation in matters of barter. It was uttered at the completion of a trade by the party who felt that he had got the better of the deal, and it meant that the agreement could not be reneged upon.

The ultimate oath in matters of honor not covered by the rules of sport or commerce was "My Jewish Word of Honor." For example:

MAURICE Tommy Lentz said that your sister was a whore.
ME You swear?
MAURICE Yeah.
ME Swear to God?
MAURICE Yeah.
ME Jewish Word of Honor?
MAURICE Yeah. (*Pause*)
ME Say it.
MAURICE I just *said* I said it.
ME Say it.
MAURICE I don't want to say "Your sister is a whore."
ME Just say he said it.
MAURICE Tommy Lentz, My Jewish Word of Honor, said your sister was a whore.

Which meant that it was so. Until that day when one discovered it was possible to swear falsely, and that there was, finally, *no* magic force of words capable of assuring the truth in oneself or in others, and so became adult and very serious and monotheistic in one hard moment.

The other morning a man came into the McBurney YMCA to run. He was told that the running track was closed until noon. He was inspired with rage that he had made a long trip to the Y and now could not run, and he was berating one of the office personnel for not putting up a sign yesterday which would have informed him that he could not run that day till noon. He wanted the clerk to say a word or phrase of explanation or apology which would have the power to have put a sign up the day before.

In his anger he had reverted to a universe where words were clearly magic, in which all things were possessed of spirit, and where anything was possible.

A NATIONAL
DREAM-LIFE

We respond to a drama to that extent to which it corresponds to our dream life.

The life of the play is the life of the unconscious, the protagonist represents ourselves, and the main action of the play constitutes the subject of the dream or myth. It is not the theme of the play to which we respond, but the *action*—the through-action of the protagonist, and the attendant support of the secondary characters, this support lent through their congruent actions.

The play is a quest for a solution.

As in our dreams, the law of psychic economy operates. In dreams we do not seek answers which our conscious (rational) mind is capable of supplying, we seek answers to those questions which the conscious mind is incompetent to deal with. So with the drama, if the question posed is one which can be answered rationally, e.g.: how does one fix a car, should white people be nice to black people, are the physically handicapped entitled to our respect, our enjoyment of the drama is incomplete—we feel diverted but not fulfilled. Only if the question posed is one whose complexity and depth renders it unsusceptible to rational examination does the dramatic treatment seem to us appropriate, and the dramatic solution become enlightening.

Ecclesiastes 9:12. "For man also knoweth not his time: as the fishes that are taken in an evil net, and as the birds that are caught in a snare; so are the sons of man snared in an evil time when it falleth suddenly upon them." The solution— which is to say solution which will enable us to function happily in the midst of rational uncertainty to a personal and seemingly unresolvable psychological problem—is the dream; the solution to a seemingly unresolvable social (ethic) problem is the drama (poem). For the sine qua non of both the dream and the drama is the suspension of rational restrictions in aid of happiness.

The American theater, acting as a collective mentality, operates in much the same way as the unconscious of the individual in the choice of topics worthy of treatment, and in the choice of treatment *of* those topics. Election by the playwright of theme, action, and so on, the extent to which the plays growing out of those elections are deemed acceptable by producers, and the choice of actors and designers are made artistically (which is to say *unconsciously*) and are based, however they may be rationalized ex post facto, on considerations which approximate those which determine the individual's choice of dream material: "Does examination of this idea, of this action, seem to offer a solution to an unconscious confusion of mine at the present time?"*

*The objection that this assertion does not take into consideration purely venal motives on the part of the producers, authors, and so on can be answered by the proposition that in an election which is apparently *completely* economic, the producer does not ask the question "Will this play offer a solution?" of *himself* but posits an imaginary individual called the Middle-Class Theatergoer and asks, if only subconsciously, "Will this play offer a solution to or 'please' such a person?" But the Middle-Class Theatergoer exists only in the producer's mind, and the concerns and desires of this chimera come from nowhere but the producer's own subconscious.

Surely individual instances of choices may not adhere to, or may even serve to mitigate against, this process, but taking the progress of the play from its inception in the unconscious of the playwright to its presentation before the public as a whole, and as a *community endeavor*, the process of collective choice is the predominant and overriding force. Through it, the artistic community (subconsciously) elects and forms our national dreams.

To the greatest extent we, in an evil time, which is to say a time in which we do not wish to examine ourselves and our unhappiness; we, in the body of the artistic community, elect dream material (plays) which cater to a very low level of fantasy. We cast ourselves (for in the writing and the production and the patronage of plays we cannot but identify with the protagonist) in dreams of wish fulfillment. These dreams—even and, perhaps, especially those which seem the most conservative and bourgeois—seem to offer solutions to our concerns based on the idea that the concerns *themselves* do not exist, that they are only temporary aberrations of an essentially benign universe, or (and here is, perhaps, the hidden delusional postulate in our election of the happy-ending comedy-drama) of a universe which is positively *responsive* at that point at which our individual worthinesses (or inabilities, as it amounts to the same thing) are brought to its attentions. We leave the theater after such plays as smug as after a satisfying daydream. Our prejudices have been assuaged, and we have been reassured that nothing is wrong, but we are, finally, no happier.

In a less evil time we are more capable as an artistic community of creating and ratifying plays (in electing for the subject of our dreams) questions concerning deeper uncertainties. We all dream each night, but at some times we are reluctant to remember our dreams; just so we, as a collective artistic unity, create poetic (theatrical) dreams, but at some times we are reluctant to remember (stage, accept, support . . .) them. Many times the true nature of our dreams is hidden from us: and just so in the Theater, the dramas elected and staged may represent an attempt at diversion or denial of our dream life. These instances may correspond, in terms of psychic economy, to a national period of inner-directedness and a hypochondriacal concern in the theater with the impedimenta of our lives (realism); or a complete and angry denial of the existence of all nonsuperficial concerns ("experimental theater").

A dramatic experience concerned with the mundane may inform but it cannot release; and one concerned essentially with the *aesthetic politics* of its creators may divert or anger, but it cannot enlighten.

As we move into a time when we as a nation once again can sense the possibility of a rational self-esteem, the theater both heralds and promotes the possibility of the greatest benefit of the reasoned self-view, an individual contentment born of balance. This possibility, at the moment, seems to exist in our national mentality and in our national theater. Freud said, "The only way to forget is to remember," and a subscription to this belief—this wish to cleanse and renew—can be seen in the current renewed interest in and reawakening of the poetic drama; and this reawakening is our national wish to remember our dreams.

RADIO DRAMA

Sunday nights we would go visiting. Coming home we'd play the car radio. It was dark and we'd be rolling through the prairies outside of Chicago. CBS "Suspense" would be on the air, or "Yours Truly, Johnny Dollar—the Man with the Million-Dollar Expense Account." And the trip home always ended too soon; we'd stay in the car until my dad kicked us out—we wanted to hear how the story ended; we wanted the trip to be endless—rolling through the prairies and listening to the intimate voices.

But we went into the house.

It never occurred to us to turn on the radio when we got in. We were the very first television generation. My dad was proud of the television, and we grew up considering the radio déclassé—it was used for information or background but not for entertainment.

We grew up with the slogans, overheard from our parents and their friends, enigmatic catchwords of their youth: "Boston Blackie, enemy to those who *make* him an enemy, friend to those who *have* no friends." "Who knows what evil lurks in the hearts of men? The *Shadow* do..." (That wonderful apocryphal transposition.) "*Gang*busters...!" "Can a young girl from Ohio find happiness..." Et cetera.

I had written a piece called "The Water Engine." It was set in 1933 Chicago, during the Century of Progress Exposition, and concerned a young man who invented an engine which ran solely on water.

I wrote it as a short story, and it was rejected by many publications. I wrote it as a movie treatment and it was rejected by various studios. I threw it in the wastebasket and, later that day, someone introduced me to Howard Gelman, who was the producer of Earplay, an outfit which commissions, produces, and distributes radio drama to the National Public Radio network.

Howard knew my playwriting from Chicago. He asked me if I wanted to write for the radio, and I said yes, went home, and got "The Water Engine" out of the wastebasket.

Earplay has since produced other plays of mine: *Reunion*, *A Sermon*, and *Prairie Du Chien*. And writing for radio I learned a lot about playwriting.

Bruno Bettelheim, in *The Uses of Enchantment*, writes that the fairy tale (and, similarly, the Drama) has the capacity to calm, to incite, to assuage, finally, to *affect*, because we listen to it nonjudgmentally—we identify *sub*consciously (noncritically) with the protagonist.

We are allowed to do this, he tells us, because the protagonist and, indeed, the *situations* are uncharacterized aside from their most essential elements.

When we are told, for example, that a Handsome Prince went into a wood, we realize that *we* are that Handsome Prince. As soon as the prince is characterized, "A Handsome Blond Prince with a twinkle in his eye, and just the hint of a mustache on his upper lip..." and if we lack that color hair, twinkle, and so on, we say, "What an interesting prince. Of course, he is unlike anyone *I* know..." and we begin to listen to the story as a *critic* rather than as a *participant*.

The essential task of the drama (as of the fairy tale) is to offer a solution to a problem which is nonsusceptible to reason. To be effective, the drama must induce us to suspend our rational judgment, and to follow the *internal* logic of the piece, so that our *pleasure* (our "cure") is the release at the end of the story. We enjoy the happiness of being a participant in the process of *solution*, rather than the intellectual achievement of having observed the process of construction.

And the best model for this drama is The Story around the Campfire.

We hear ". . . a windswept moor" and immediately supply the perfect imaginary moor. And the moor we supply is not perfect "in general," but perfect according to our subconscious understanding of the significance of the moor *to the story*.

This is why radio is a great training ground for dramatists. More than any other dramatic medium it teaches the writer to concentrate on the essentials, because it throws into immediate relief that to *characterize* the people or scene is to take time from the story—to weaken the story. Working for radio, I learned the way *all* great drama works: by leaving the *endowment* of characters, place, and especially action up to the audience. Only by eschewing the desire to *characterize* can one begin to understand the model of the perfect play.

The model of the perfect play is the dirty joke.

"Two guys go into a farmhouse. An old woman is stirring a pot of soup."

What does the woman look like? What state is the farmhouse in? Why is she stirring soup? It is absolutely not important. The dirty-joke teller is tending toward a punch line and we know that he or she is only going to tell us the elements which direct our attention *toward* that punch line, so we listen attentively and gratefully.

Good drama has no stage directions. It is the interaction of the characters' objectives expressed *solely* through what they *say* to each other—not through what the author says *about* them. The better the play, the better it will fare on the radio. Put *Streetcar, Waiting for Godot, Long Day's Journey, Lear* on the radio, and what do you miss? Nothing.

Our enjoyment is *increased* by the absence of the merely
descriptive. (A note here, as long as I have the forum, to
beginning playwrights. A lesson from radio: don't write stage
directions. If it is not apparent what the character is trying
to accomplish by saying the line, telling us *how* the character
said it, or whether or not she moved to the couch isn't going
to aid the case. We might understand better what the character
means but we aren't particularly going to *care*.)

In *An Actor Prepares*, Stanislavsky is asked by a student
actor how, faced with all the myriad choices open to an actor
onstage, Stanislavsky always manages to make the correct
choice, a choice which puts forward the play. He responds
that once on a Volga steamer he approached the captain and
asked how, when faced with the myriad decisions involved
in navigating such a dangerous river, the captain always managed to make the correct choice. The captain, he tells us,
replied, "I stick to the channel." So, Stan tells the student,
"Stick to the channel and you cannot be wrong. The choices
that you make will not be 'in general,' but in aid of the story,
and, so, they must be correct."

Writing for radio forces you and *teaches* you to stick to the
channel, which is to say, the *story*. The *story* is all there is
to the theater—the rest is just packaging, and that is the
lesson of radio.

Stan Freberg, a fiendishly inventive writer, once did a radio
commercial for radio advertising, a dialogue between a television and a radio ad exec. The radio exec says, "Here's my
ad: You take Lake Michigan and drain it. Bombers of the
Royal Canadian Air Force fly over, laden with whipped cream.
They drop the whipped cream in the lake until the lake is
full. A huge helicopter circles Chicago carrying a forty-five-
ton cherry and drops it on the top of the whipped cream, as
the tops of the Chicago skyscrapers explode and paint the
evening sky with fireworks from horizon to horizon. Do that
on TV."

Broadway theater by no means withstanding, the best production is the *least* production. The best production takes place in the mind of the beholder.

We, as audience, are much better off with a sign that says A BLASTED HEATH, than with all the brilliant cinematography in the world. To say "brilliant cinematography" is to say, "He made the trains run on time."

Witness the rather fascistic trend in cinema in the last decade.

Q. How'd you like the movie?

A. Fantastic cinematography.

Yeah, but so what? Hitler had fantastic cinematography. The question we have ceased to ask is, "What was the fantastic or brilliant cinematography in *aid* of?"

As "fantastic cinematography" has been the death of the American film, "production" has been the death of the American theater.

"Production" or "production values" is code for *forsaking the story*. "Production values" is a term invented by what used to be called "angels" when they were in the theater to meet members of the chorus, and who are now called producers, and God *knows* why they are in the theater.

Writing for the radio teaches there is no such thing as "production values." The phrase means "Pour money on it," and it has been the ruin of television, movies, and the professional stage. It is The Triumph of the General—The Celebration of Nothing to Say.

If Mount St. Helens could fit in a theater some producer would suggest teaming it with Anthony Hopkins and doing *Huey*. *That* is "production values."

But radio drama, God bless it, needs inventive actors, an inventive sound-effects person, and a good script. You can produce it for next to nothing. The writer and the actor can both practice and perfect their trade away from the countervailing influence of producers, critics, and money; and if it doesn't work they can do another one just as simply and cheaply without ruining either their career or a large hunk of risk capital which might have meant an addition to the house in Larchmont.

Martin Esselin helped reinvent the British drama as head of BBC Radio Drama after World War II by commissioning Pinter, Joe Orton, and others. He helped re-create a national theater by *enfranchising creative talent*. In the same way Howard Gelman of Earplay, in commissioning Wendy Wasserstein, Terry Curtis Fox, Romulus Linney, Lanford Wilson, and so on, is supporting the American theater in the best way: by encouraging freedom of thought—by hiring the writers and letting them be free.

We live in oppressive times. We have, as a nation, become our own thought police; but instead of calling the process by which we limit our expression of dissent and wonder "censorship," we call it "concern for commercial viability."

Whatever we call it, it *is* censorship. It is curtailment of freedom of speech and of imagination, and, as Tolstoy says, this oppression, as usual, is committed in the name of public tranquillity.

How different is saying, "It would create public unrest," from saying, "It's not going to sell. They aren't going to *buy* it"?

It's hard to find a Great American Play on Broadway. It's getting too expensive to produce. To mount a three-character, one-set drama costs around $750,000, and the people with the money aren't going to put it up to enjoy a *succès d'estime*. They're putting it up in the hopes it is going to *make* money, which means they are doing everything in their power to appeal to the *widest possible* audience, which makes it difficult for a play to be produced that *questions, investigates*, and so, probably, *disturbs*.

Similarly with the movies. They aren't administered by Miss Dove, but by people interested solely in making a buck on the buck they have put out. And television people who put out a news special on nuns being trampled to death by elephants would turn it into a series if the viewer response were great enough. These media (and we might as well include publishing) have, in an introverted time, become self-censoring—and they refer to the process not as thought policing but as cost accounting.

But radio is inexpensive to produce. God bless it—the essential nature of the form is that it *suffers immediately* from the addition of production values, just as would a dirty joke (when you introduce the Farmer's Daughter you don't put your hair in braids to illustrate). Radio drama can be produced by anybody with a microphone and a tape recorder. The time is auspicious for a rebirth of American Theater, and radio would be a good place to look for it to happen.

A TRADITION OF THE
THEATER AS ART

We are told the theater is al-
ways dying. And it's true, and, rather than being decried, it
should be understood. The theater is an expression of our
dream life—of our unconscious aspirations.

It responds to that which is best, most troubled, most
visionary in our society. As the society changes, the theater
changes.

Our workers in the theater—actors, writers, directors,
teachers—are drawn to it not out of intellectual predilection,
but from *necessity*. We are driven into the theater by our need
to express—our need to answer the questions of our lives—
the questions of the time in which we live. Of this moment.

The theatrical artist serves the same function in society
that dreams do in our subconscious life—the subconscious
life of the individual. We are elected to supply the dreams
of the body politic—we are the dream makers of the society.

What we act out, design, write, springs not from mean-
ingless individual fancy, but from the soul of the times—that
soul both observed by and expressed *in* the artist.

The artist is the advance explorer of the societal consciousness. As such, many times his first reports are disbe-
lieved.

Later those reports may be acclaimed and then, perhaps, enshrined, which is to say sterilized—deemed descriptive not of an outward reality, but of the curious and idiosyncratic mental state of the artist. Later still the reports, and the artist, may be discarded as so commonplace as to be useless.

It is not the theater which is dying, but men and women—society. And as it dies a new group of explorers, artists, arises whose reports are disregarded, then enshrined, then disregarded.

The theater is always dying because artistic inspiration cannot be instilled—it can only be nurtured.

Most theatrical institutions survive creatively only for one generation. When the necessity which gave rise to them is gone, all that is left is the shell. The codification of a vision—which is no vision at all.

The artistic urge—the urge to create—becomes the institutional urge—the urge to *preserve*. The two are antithetical.

What can be preserved? What can be communicated from one generation to the next?

Philosophy. Morality. Aesthetics.

These can be expressed in technique, in those skills which enable the artist to respond truthfully, fully, lovingly to whatever he or she wishes to express.

These skills—the skills of the theater—cannot be communicated intellectually. They must be learned firsthand in long practice under the tutelage of someone who learned them firsthand. They must be learned from an artist.

The skills of the theater must be learned in practice with, and in emulation of, those capable of employing them.

This is what can and must be passed from one generation to the next. Technique—a knowledge of how to translate inchoate desire into clean action—into action capable of communicating itself to the audience.

This technique, this care, this love of precision, of cleanliness, this love of the theater, is the best way, for it is love of the *audience*—of that which *unites* the actor and the house: a desire to share something which they know to be true.

Without technique, which is to say without philosophy, acting cannot be art. And if it cannot be art, we are in serious trouble.

We live in an illiterate country. The mass media—the commercial theater included—pander to the low and the lowest of the low in the human experience. They, finally, debase us through the sheer weight of their mindlessness.

Every reiteration of the idea that *nothing matters* debases the human spirit.

Every reiteration of the idea that there is no drama in modern life, there is only dramatization, that there is no tragedy, there is only unexplained misfortune, debases us. It denies what we know to be true. In denying what we know, we are as a nation which cannot remember its dreams—like an unhappy person who cannot remember his dreams and so denies that he *does* dream, and denies that there are such things as dreams.

We are destroying ourselves by accepting our unhappiness.

We are destroying ourselves by endorsing an acceptance of oblivion in television, motion pictures, and the stage.

Who is going to speak up? Who is going to speak for the American spirit? For the human spirit?

Who is capable of being heard? Of being accepted? Of being believed? Only that person who speaks without ulterior motives, without hope of gain, without even the desire to *change*, with only the desire to *create*: The artist. The actor. The strong, trained actor dedicated to the idea that the theater is the place we go to hear the truth, and equipped with the technical capacity to speak simply and clearly.

If we expect the actor, the theatrical artist, to have the strength to say no to television, to say no to that which debases, and to say yes to the stage—to that stage which is the proponent of the life of the soul—that actor is going to have to be trained, and endorsed, *concretely* for his efforts.

People cannot be expected to put aside even the meager comfort of financial success and critical acclaim (or the even more meager—and more widespread—comfort of the *hope* of those) unless they can be *shown* something *better.*

We must support each other *concretely* in the quest for artistic knowledge, in the struggle to create.

We must support each other in the things we say, in the things we choose to produce, in the things we choose to attend, in the things we choose to endow.

Only active choices on our parts will take theater, *true* theater, noncommercial theater, out of the realm of *good works*, and place it in the realm of art—an art whose benefits will cheer us, and will warm us, and will care for us, and elevate our soul out of these sorry times.

We have the opportunity now to *create* a new theater—and to endorse a *tradition* in theater, a tradition of true creation.

There is a story that a student once came to Evgeny Vakhtangov, an actor of the Moscow Art Theatre who founded his own studio to direct and to teach, and said, "Vakhtangov, you work so hard and with so little reward. You should have your own theater."

Vakhtangov replied, "You know who had his own theater? Anton Chekhov."

"Yes," the student said, "Chekhov had the Art Theatre, the Moscow Art Theatre."

"No," said Vakhtangov, "I mean that Chekhov had his *own* theater. The Theater which he carried in his heart, and which he alone saw."

Sanford Meisner's greatness is that for fifty years he has been training and preparing people to work in a theater which he alone saw—which existed only in his heart.

The results of his efforts are seen in the fact of the Neighborhood Playhouse School, the work of his students, and in the beginning of the Playhouse Repertory Company.

Many of us are here tonight in partial fulfillment of a debt to Mr. Meisner and more, importantly, to the same tradition to which he owes a debt—the tradition of Theater as Art.

The tradition of the theater as the place we can go to hear the truth.

FIRST PRINCIPLES

The proclamation and repetition of first principles is a constant feature of life in our democracy. Active adherence to these principles, however, has always been considered un-American.

We recipients of the boon of liberty have always been ready, when faced with discomfort, to discard any and all first principles of liberty, and, further, to indict those who do not freely join with us in happily arrogating those principles.

Freedom of speech, religion, and sexual preference are tolerated only until their exercise is found offensive, at which point those freedoms are haughtily revoked—and we hear, "Yes, but the framers of the Constitution," or Christ, or Lincoln, or whatever saint we are choosing to invoke in our support, "surely didn't envision an instance as extreme as *this*."

We tolerate and repeat the teachings of Christ, but explain that the injunction against murder surely cannot be construed to apply to *war*, and that against theft does not apply to *commerce*. We sanctify the Constitution of the United States, but explain that freedom of choice is meant to apply to all except women, racial minorities, homosexuals, the poor, opponents of the government, and those with whose ideas we disagree.

The Theater also has its First Principles—principles which make our presentations honest, moral, and, coincidentally, moving, funny, and worth the time and money of the audience.

Most of us are acquainted with these theatrical rules, which subjugate all aspects of the production to the *idea* of the play, and cause all elements to adhere to and *express* that idea forcefully, fully, without desire for praise or fear of censure. But, in the first moment of difficulty with our work we, many times, assure ourselves that principles of unity, simplicity, and honesty are well and good under normal circumstances, but we surely cannot be meant to apply them under the extraordinary pressures of actually working on a play.

We discard our first principles at the moment they cause us unpleasantness—when they might send the author back for another draft, or the piece back for another week or month of rehearsal, or cause the director to work on a scene until it is finished, or cause a producer to say, "You know, on reflection this piece is garbage. I think it would be better for all concerned if we didn't put it on."

. . . Yes, but we have seats to fill, we have to get on to the next act, we have a deadline to meet.

If we act as if the Aristotelian Unities, the philosophy of Stanislavsky, or Brecht, or Shaw, were effete musings, and intended for some ideal theater, and not applicable to our own work, we are declining the responsibility for *creating* that ideal theater.

Every time an actor deviates from the through-line of a piece (that is, the first principle of the piece) for whatever reason—to gain praise, or out of laziness, or because he hasn't taken the time to discover how that one difficult moment actually *expresses* the through-line, he creates in himself the habit of moral turpitude; and the *play*, which is a strict lesson in ethics, is given the lie.

Every time the author leaves in a piece of nonessential prose (beautiful though it may be), he weakens the structure of the play, and, again, the audience learns *this* lesson: no one is taking responsibility: theater people are prepared to *espouse* a moral act, but not to *commit* it.

When we deviate from first principles we communicate to the audience a lesson in cowardice. This lesson is of as great a magnitude as our subversion of the Constitution by involvement in Vietnam, in Ford's pardon of Nixon, in the persecution of the Rosenbergs, in the reinstatement of the death penalty. They are all lessons in cowardice, and each begets cowardice.

Alternatively, the theater affords an opportunity uniquely suited for communicating and inspiring ethical behavior: the audience is given the possibility of seeing live people onstage carrying out an action based on first principles (these principles being the objectives of the play's protagonists) and carrying this action to its full conclusion.

The audience then participates at a celebration of the idea that Intention A begets Result B. The audience imbibes that lesson as regards the given circumstances of the play, and they *also* receive the lesson as regards the standards of production, writing, acting, design, and direction.

If theatrical workers are seen *not* to have the courage of their convictions (which is to say, the courage to relegate every aspect of production to the laws of theatrical action, economy, and, specifically, the requirements of the superobjective of the play), the audience, once again, learns a lesson in moral cowardice, and we add to the burden of their lives. We add to their loneliness.

Each time we try to subordinate all we do to the necessity of bringing to life simply and completely the intention of the play, we give the audience an experience which enlightens and frees them: the experience of witnessing their fellow human beings saying, "Nothing will sway me, nothing will divert me, nothing will dilute my intention of achieving what I have sworn to achieve": in technical terms, "My Objective"; in general terms, my "goal," my "desire," my "responsibility."

The theatrical repetition of this lesson can and *will* in time help teach that it is possible and *pleasant* to substitute action for inaction, courage for cowardice, humanity for selfishness.

If we hold to those first principles of action and beauty and economy which we know to be true, and hold to them in *all* things—choice of plays, method of actor training, writing, advertising, promotion—we can *uniquely* speak to our fellow citizens.

In a morally bankrupt time we can help to change the habit of coercive and frightened action and substitute for it the habit of trust, self-reliance, and cooperation.

If we are true to our ideals we can help to form an ideal society—a society based on and adhering to ethical first principles—not by *preaching* about it, but by *creating* it each night in front of the audience—by showing how it works. In action.

STANISLAVSKY AND THE
AMERICAN BICENTENNIAL

There is a homily popularly attributed to the Chinese to the effect that the time one spends fishing is not deducted from one's life span. This may or may not be true of fishing (I for one am not at all loath to believe in a universe ruled by aesthetically pleasing ideas rather than immutable laws) but it is certainly not true of the theater. The time one spends in a theater—whether as spectator or as worker—is deducted from one's total allotment, and this is what Stanislavsky had in mind when he said, "Play well, or play badly, but play truly."

Stanislavsky recognized that the Theater is a part of one's total life experience, that it is an environment wherein human beings interact (where they breathe together, the actors and the audience), and that not only the physical and psychological, but also the *ethical* laws of life on the stage are no different than those on the street. The theater is not an imitation of anything, it is real theater.

Stanislavsky's art, his humanism, his great gift to world theater, was the recognition that on the stage, just as in the office or the supermarket or the school, human beings must concern themselves with the truth of the individual moment, and recognize and ratify their coconspirators' existence and desire.

Tolstoy was the major philosophical influence on Stanislavsky, and Tolstoy's dictum "If you cannot deal with Human Beings with love, you must not deal with them at all" is the *a priori* of the work of Stanislavsky and his colleagues and his students and their students.

Stanislavsky's ideas, basically philosophic rather than technical, are generally known as the Stanislavsky System, and posit the theater primarily as a place of recognition and ratification. Implicit in the Stanislavsky System is the idea that human beings are infinitely perfectible, and always strive to do good—to the limit of their ability and according to their best lights. (This concept is embodied in the technical sphere in the idea of *objective*.)

The theater must be a place where mutual recognition of this desire can take place. The artist must avow humanity in him- or herself, and also in the audience. (Many theatrical artisans have an incorrect or incomplete, but in any case, unhappy, understanding of the relationship between themselves and the audience. The misunderstanding exists for many unfortunate reasons, not the least of which is the general low esteem in which the theatrical artisan is held and learns to hold him- or herself.)

In the theater we must strive to recognize and to ratify the universality of our desires and our fears as human beings. If we continue to shove them under the rug—our anxieties and also our joys—if we continue to lose a basis for comparison (and, with it, a rational self-image), we will continue to live in an unhappy land.

"Play well, or play badly, but play truly." Try as one might, one cannot escape the temporal exigencies; all the polish in the world will not mitigate the fact of Death or the reality of a mutable universe. You can't make it so pretty that it goes away, all you can do is live the moment fully and *avow* the finite and fleeting nature of consciousness.

The theater is not a place where one should go to forget, but rather a place where one should go to remember.

Just as the act of making love can and should be made a spiritual act by an avowal of the transient nature of the body, just so the theatrical experience must be an *adoration* of the *evanescent*, a celebration of the transient nature of individual life (and, perhaps, through this, a glimpse at some less-transient realities).

The magic moments, the beautiful moments in the theater always come from a desire on the part of artist *and* audience to live in the moment—to *commit* themselves to time.

Kafka wrote that one always has the alternative of ignoring and choosing not to participate in the sufferings of others, but that in so doing one commits oneself to the only suffering that one could have avoided.

We live in an unhappy nation. As a people we are burdened with a terrible self-image. As a theatrical worker, I perceive that one way to alleviate the moral pall and the jejune supersophistication of our lives is by theatrical celebration of those things which bind us together.

I, personally, had a very rewarding week last week. I finally went to see *Three Women* at Victory Gardens, and *Our Town* at the Goodman, and I left each feeling much better than when I went in. I thought: isn't it the truth: people are born, love, hate, are frightened and happy, grow old and die. We as audience and we as artists must work to bring about a theater, an American Theater, which will be a celebration of these things.

AN UNHAPPY FAMILY

In the American Theater *status*—the ability to extract deference from others—is automatically conferred on the basis of a set hierarchy—on the basis of *job title*.

The actor is manipulated and controlled by the director, who is similarly in thrall to the producer. The unquestioned acceptance of this "Great Chain of Being" is based on the fiction that it is "good for the production." But any reasonable person in the theater sees this is seldom the case, and so the conscious acceptance of this hierarchy ("It's good for the production and I better shut up or I'll lose my job") is coupled with a deep, deep anger.

Those down the chain seem to have two choices: they may accept an idealized version of those over them: ("I don't know or like what they're up to, but—on the basis of their credits and their position—I can only assume that they are right and I am wrong"); or they may rebel, fume, gossip, and plot— much as if those in control were their parents—which is precisely what this relationship recapitulates ... that of the child to the parent.

This paternalistic pattern in the theater infantilizes the

actors, so they feel compelled to please rather than to create, to rebel rather than to explore, to perform rather than to express.

As in the parent-child relationship, the motive for control in the theater is always stated as The Good of the Child. "I, as producer, director, must *ignore* your questions about the worth of this piece of blocking/piece of direction/piece of dramaturgy. My word is law, it is for your own good to obey unthinkingly, and if you begin to doubt and question me, the havoc you cause will destroy all the good I am trying to do for you and your colleagues."

In the family, as in the theater, the urge to control only benefits the controller. Blind obedience saves him the onerous duty of examining his preconceptions, his *own* wisdom, and, finally, *his own worth*.

The desire to manipulate, to treat one's colleagues as servants, reveals a deep sense of personal worthlessness: as if one's personal thoughts, choices, and insights could not bear reflection, let alone a reasoned mutual examination.

Members of a healthy theater/family treat each other with respect and love; and those who know better *do* better, knowing that those who love them will strive to emulate them.

In a meritocracy, status and the power to direct the actions of others would, at least, be won by demonstration of excellence and *some* form of communal assent. But in *our* theater, in *our* unhappy family, those who come in "last," who come in "at the bottom"—the actors—are subject to the unreasoned, unloving, and frightened whims of those in (financial) power over them. They are the new baby born to oppressed parents who *finally* have someone to control.

In both situations the recipient of this control is made to fear for his livelihood—for his very life—if he does not obey unquestioningly, and so is robbed of his dignity.

This unreasoned commercial hierarchy of actor-director-producer has drained the theater of its most powerful force: the phenomenal strength and generosity of the actor; and, as in any situation of unhappy tryanny, the oppressed must free the oppressor.

SOME THOUGHTS ON
WRITING IN RESTAURANTS

In a restaurant one is both ob-
served and unobserved. Joy and sorrow can be displayed and
observed "unwittingly," the writer scowling naively and the
diners wondering, What the *hell* is he doing? Then, again,
the writer may be *truly* unobserved, which affects not a jot
the scourge of popular opinion on his overactive mind.

Couples play out scenes in restaurants. The ritual of acting
out and displaying changes in one's state before the tribe has
disappeared, but the urge lives on; and the ritual of dissolution
of the affaire in a restaurant is strong and compelling now when
the marriage ceremony has become an empty form.

One might say the urge to participate in the ritual is almost
irresistible because it cures, cleanses, and assures. The man
stands in a restaurant and testifies before his peers (and what
better place to locate them than in a restaurant?). "I'm *trying*
and I call on you all to witness me. I am not bad, but good;
for I would not dissolve this union without your blessing."
He is the carny operator riding solo on the carousel to dissolve
his union, the Indian squaw putting her husband's moccasins
outside the tepee.

True ritual evolves spontaneously in and among those with
a community of interests. As the Fourth of July, Christmas,

and Chanukah no longer meet our needs and we begin to celebrate them with a *mauvaise honte*, the rituals of screaming at an unpopular choice of the Academy Awards, of shrieking disbelief when your guy catches the long one in the end zone become stronger—for the involuntary "Goddamn that man can throw" is just "Allah Akbar," in twentieth-century urban clothing. Deny them as we may, we still need the gods.

"Is God dead?" and "Why are there no real movies anymore?" are pretty much the same question. They both mean that our symbols and our myths have failed us—that we have begun to take them literally, and so judge them wanting.

In taking those questions as anything more than rhetorical, it is as if we are saying, "I am going to stay up all night and *prove* to you that no white-haired man is going to come down the chimney."

We want to see movie stars' genitals on-screen and to be assured that "they did their own stunts." We are asking Christ to throw himself down from the building.

When we demand a rational and immediately practical translation of rituals, we deny their unconscious purpose and power; we, in effect, reject our own power to solve problems— to deal with the abstract. So doing, we are forced to ignore those problems incapable of immediate, rational solutions. As these are the problems most important in our life, by denying their existence we create deep personal and communal anxiety.

Most of our communal anxiety is treated in the low level (low level because it is not cathartic but analgesic—it does not cleanse, but merely puts off) ritual of television.

Television is the whipping boy elected to suffer our emotions; it is the husband in the African tribe who undergoes the labor pains, as to have the wife undergo them would be too debilitating.

So television ritualizes our disapproval (of the Polish government), our grief (at the memorial anniversary of Dr. King, or Robert Kennedy), and our joy (when Billie finds her Lost

Dog). None of these subjects actually has the power to elicit the emotions television supposes to treat, so its supposed *treatment* of them is nothing other than nostalgia for the capacity to be involved.

But the writer elects himself to suffer the emotions society disavows; the act of creation, no less than the final production, when suffered in public gives to the lone creator the satisfaction of fulfilling a place in society.

Policemen so cherish their status as keepers of the peace and protectors of the public that they have occasionally been known to beat to death those citizens or groups who question that status.

The urge to support each other's social position has atrophied, much as architecture has degenerated in a time of buildings too large for reference to the human scale. Where the individual cannot compare himself to the group, he cannot compare his achievements to the achievements of the group.

As the Victorians assiduously expunged reference to sex, so we expunge direct reference to that which *we* desire most, which is love and a sense of belonging.

The writer sits at a two-top near the window in the restaurant. The sound of traffic just might mimic a mother's heartbeat and the Muzak plays love songs the true meaning of which can be simply found by replacing the word "you" every time it appears in the lyrics, with the word "I."

Through these manufactured perverted songs and their counterparts in television, movies, and publishing, we express love much as we express chagrin: over those things which cannot reciprocate and, further, over those things whose acceptability *as a love object* is absolutely incontrovertibly safe: we have ritualized the expression of love and limited its objects to other men's wives (in country music); the past and the future (in movies); and in television, puppets.

Movie stars have idiosyncrasies. They exist on screen and off; they are subject, on screen and off, to the same unacceptable urges that confront us all, so they have been replaced in the public estimation by Miss Piggy, E.T., the Muppets—constructions incapable of spontaneity and so of inspiration—a ritualized celebration of (what greater example?) the Absence of Will as a laudable state.

Some tribe in the future, far in the future, might find a pistol, perhaps the world's last pistol, and one hundred rounds of ammunition. The priests of that tribe, in tribute to the unknown, might invent a holiday and fire one bullet each year as a link to the unknown. After ninety years, it isn't difficult to imagine that a new bull might be put forth that shots were to be fired only every *hundred* years, at the expiration of which time the something extraordinary might be foreseen to occur.

And perhaps at the expiration of nine hundred years a new bull might go forth to the effect that the last round never was to be expended—that the tribe would choose to worship *potentiality* in their artifacts rather than uselessness.

But *our* tribe has fired the last round and our only link to the possibility of powers greater than ourselves is the useless gun, the essential element we no longer possess. And since our priests have fired off that last round, they have expanded any possible link to the past, as such a memory would surely cause us pain. Therefore, our dead rituals are rituals of denial. They concern not potential but *lack*, and express contempt—contempt, mainly for ourselves, and for our urge to celebrate.

Let's look elsewhere. Not in the shul and in the church; their time has passed—though it will come again. The human urge to celebrate, which is to say the reemergence of religion, the reemergence of the involuntary, and that which tends toward release and reaffirmation, will be seen to reassert itself in the profane, commonplace, and pagan aspects of our lives, in the scorn heaped on the Academy Awards committee that we cannot dare attribute rightfully to *government;* the ritual suggestion of sodomy in "take this job and shove it"; the ritual of the fire department's dog; the writer in the restaurant; the adopted southern accent of airline pilots; the exclamation of awe at the long run up the middle. These unproclaimed but operative rituals are meager, but they are close to all we have of spiritual community—they have replaced the awe of the sacrament, which itself replaced the miracle of rebirth from the dead.

PART II

∎

EXUVIAL MAGIC

EXUVIAL MAGIC:
AN ESSAY CONCERNING
FASHION

The pursuit of Fashion is the attempt of the middle class to co-opt tragedy.

In adopting the clothing, speech, and personal habits of those in straitened, dangerous, or pitiful circumstances, the middle class seeks to have what it feels to be the exigent and nonequivocal experiences had by those it emulates.

In progressing from an emulation of the *romantic* to an emulation of the *tragic*, the middle class unconsciously avows not only the aridity of its lifestyle, but the complete failure of its fantasies, and of its very ability to fantasize.

We dress in the denim of the farm worker and the prisoner of the state, the olive drab and khaki of the field soldier, the gray and blue of the Chinese laborer, the beaten leather jackets of the breadline.

The white world tries to emulate the black world; the straight world takes its fashions straight from gay society. The gay world, in its preoccupation with the *chic* of the banal, of the *passé*, of *gaucherie*, emulates those elements of the America it considers tragic—the clothing of the 1950s. So with black emulation and exaggeration of the fashion of suburbia—the Cadillac El Dorado, the color-coordinated shirt and tie and suit.

In contemporary plastic art much attention is paid to the

artist capable of making a completely obtuse statement. The middle class sneers at the analytical and exults the occult. The very fact of something being beyond the experience of the middle class is sufficient to ratify that something in its eyes. In pursuing the tragic we gainsay our own too-sad intelligence, our increasingly worthless common sense, in favor of that which is beyond our experience and, therefore, *possibly* productive.

Our preoccupation with personalities—particularly the personalities of artists—is another manifestation of our frantic search for nonequivocal experience. The product of the artist has become less important than the *fact* of the artist. We wish to absorb this person. We wish to devour someone who has experienced the tragic. In our society this person is much more important than anything he might create.

We are like warriors of old who, upon vanquishing our opponent, must rip the warm heart from his body and immediately eat it, and thus absorb his strength. The eating of the heart is a very real attempt to understand. The adoption of the tragic as fashionable is the same attempt to understand through imitative magic. "What," we ask, "*is* it that gives these people—our opponents—strength?" Additionally, we know that only by taking on the most private characteristics of those we fear can we be assured of having unconditionally subdued them.

The *chic* of the summer dress of the last several years—baggy pants, bowling shirts, socks and sandals, Hawaiian shirts, sun visors—seems to have been an unconscious recognition of the generation of the fifties as a time of great confusion, fear, and national self-loathing; as a time of tragedy. So the middle class comes to recognize the tragic in itself.

We might regularly scrutinize fashion magazines, to see what class or group is being envied, and who lies in danger of becoming understood, and to what extent we members of the middle class have come to recognize ourselves.

TRUE STORIES
OF BITCHES

The bitchiest person I know is my sister. She lives in Des Plaines, Illinois—which she refers to as "The City of Destiny."

One evening in said city we were out drowning our sorrows at a delicatessen, and I said of my pastrami sandwich, "How can we eat this food? This is *heart*-attack food . . . how can we eat this?"

"Listen," she remonstrated, "it gave six million Jews the strength to resist Hitler."

And there you have the difference between talent and genius. In a few impromptu words, my sister managed to malign me, the pastrami, restaurant goers of like tastes, and six million innocent victims.

Why? Because I ate a pastrami sandwich? Not exactly, as she, too, was eating a similar sandwich. All of the above incurred my sister's wrath because I had the bad taste to express an opinion.

"You are a fool," she was saying, "you are a fool to be eating food you disapprove of. Your inability to rule your life according to your perceptions is an unfortunate trait and, doubtless, it was in some wise responsible for the murder of the European Jewry. They, although they unfortunately couldn't be here to defend themselves, were most likely equally foolish in submitting by degrees to a deathlike oppression—much as you submit to that sandwich—and *I* am a fool for sitting here with you."

When we were younger, my sister put my stepsister up to calling me on the phone and pretending to be a friend of a friend from college who was smitten with me and would like to meet me for a drink. An affable chap, I acquiesced, and heard, and still hear twenty years later, the giggles of the two girls over the phone.

Often, when speaking of completely unrelated topics, my sister will ask if I remember the time I invited my own stepsister out for a drink; and then, honor being what it is, I riposte by asking if she remembers the time her boyfriend drowned in the bathtub. His death was elevated from the unfortunate to the remarkable by the fact that he drowned in the bathtub while testing out his new scuba gear; and reference to his passing tends to cap the argument, as being the ne plus ultra of response, which is to say, bitchiness. Similarly, in husband-and-wife arguments, or, as they are generally known, "marriage," the ultimate response the man feels is, of course, physical violence. People can say what they will, we men think, but if I get pushed just one little step further, why I might, I might just ———(FILL IN THE BLANK) because she seems to have forgotten that I'M STRONGER THAN HER.

And there you have the *raison d'être* of bitchiness and its identification as a feminine tactic. We've all got to have an ace in the hole when dealing with those who are stronger.

My wife, in the whirlwind early years of our marriage, disapproved of my playing poker. Looking back, it occurs to me that she felt I should have found her exclusive company sufficient, and indeed I would have, but she didn't play poker.

Many times she would resort to a cunning and wily ruse to lure me back home from my game. She would call, for example, and say that she was down the road at the filling station, as she had forgotten the keys to the house, and would I please come home. She once called me to ask me to come home because she was scared. "Why are you scared?" I asked. "Because there's a bat in the toilet," she said.

Man that I am, I resisted her blandishments, and, on arrival home, found that there was indeed a bat in the toilet. It was a rather junior bat and had folded its wings and gone to sleep on the floor behind the bathtub, and so I nodded my head and said, "Well..."

Speaking of which: once my wife called and spoke to me thus: "Why don't you come home? Why don't you leave that silly game and come home to a woman who loves you?" If my memory serves me, her voice became somewhat husky at this point, and lower in pitch, and she said, "You know I can't sleep unless you come home." Well, I hung up the phone and I thought. I looked at my stack of chips and, as I seemed to be winning, I said to my companions, "Fellas, I'm sorry, but I have to go home."

I went home, I entered my house humming to myself, and sprinted up the stairs, loosening my clothing. My wife was fast asleep. I rubbed the small of her back. "Wake up, honey," I said or somesuch. "Mffff," she said. "Sleeping." I paused. "Yes, but," I said, "you said come home, 'cause you couldn't sleep if I'm not here." "Well, you're *here*," she said and went back to sleep.

So you see what I mean.

The culmination of which came one night when I had come home from the game quite late, and with less money that I went out with. My wife, at this point, was awake and took it up with me, my playing poker. Things escalated, as things do, and finally she shouted, "All right, if it's so important to you, just *leave*. Just leave, and never come back."

"All right," I said. And she stormed out and I got out my suitcase and started throwing versatile items of clothing into it. Boys, my mind was racing: I was free at last. I would play poker every night, and smoke cigars right in the house. I would look up all of those New York gals who understand what "freedom" means, I would live in Cheap Hotels. She came back in the room, "And take the kid," she said, and thrust our sleeping two-year-old daughter at me and walked out. There it is again: I thought I was winning. I thought I had won, and what was I left with? A very difficult form of behavior to negotiate with, that is, "I don't understand the *rules*, but I'm so nutsy that I might do anything. . . ."

I put the kid back to sleep and meditated that no one forced me to get married.

A further story of me and my wife:

One night by the fire she asked me, "Who was the most famous person that you ever slept with?" I was stunned. My wife is a genteel and sensitive woman, and that question, even in the protected intimacy of marriage, seemed crass and invasive. "Oh, honey," I said, "ha-ha-ha," and went back to my reading. "Who was the most famous person you ever slept with?" she repeated. I asked if I looked like the type who'd kiss and tell, and she said, yes, I did. After some bantering— me truly on the defensive, as I couldn't figure out what prompted this out-of-character question—I hit on a response: "Okay," I said, "who was the most famous person *you* ever slept with?" She responded instantly with a name. There now I have you, I thought, "Him?" I said. "Him??? *He* was the most famous person that you ever slept with? You slept with *him*? That lox . . . are you *joking*? Ha-ha-ha!" And limitless was my mirth for some minutes, as I expounded on her lack of taste and choice.

When I'd run down, she said, "All right, now your turn: who is the most famous person *you've* ever slept with?" There was a slight pause, I lowered my eyes, and said demurely, "All right, I slept with———." There was a moment's silence and my wife said, "Who . . . ?" As Tolstoy tells us: mediocrity sees nothing higher than itself, but talent recognizes genius instantly. People say that Bruce Lee was killed by the Touch of Death, a martial technique so occult and so advanced its adepts, with a simple touch to an unspecified part of the body, can reverse the vital mechanism and bring about death within twenty-four hours.

My mother knew and would do the usual required dressage of forgetting the names of girls of whom she did not approve, complaining that I had missed events whose existence she had neglected to inform me of, and so on. But she had one technique which, even though I was its victim, filled me with admiration.

It was in a period of my life when I was doing a lot of traveling—commuting between New York, California, and our home in Vermont.

On my stops in Chicago, we would have a fine dinner at my mother's house, and discuss the lives of various members of the family who were fortuitously not present; for example, my sister and her boyfriend who had gone to both Davy Jones and Kohler of Kohler simultaneously, and so on.

After dinner as I rose to leave, my mother would do the modern equivalent of "take a little something for the train." She would present me with a token to be taken home to commemorate the odd intervening birthday or anniversary. This was a charming habit of a charming woman, and my joy in the gift was dissipated only by the fact that I was invariably traveling light and in the midst of a flying visit to five cities, and the gift was invariably a Staffordshire serving platter. So there I was. Evening after evening. On the sidewalk outside her house—my go-getter shoulder bag with a notebook and a toothbrush and a spare pair of socks, and my arms endeavoring to protect this three-foot confection of spun porcelain.

Now, you couldn't *check* it, you couldn't carry it on the plane unless you held it in your lap, and *then* it was odds on to break. The most intelligent course would be, of course, to throw it in the trash, but HOW COULD ONE ACT LIKE THAT TO ONE'S MOTHER? And so, lashed to this fragile anchor, one thought about one's mother for the length of the trip. What did one think? *Surely* she must know ... *surely* she could have sent home a nice antique pillbox ... *surely* some part of her must know I'm going to have to dedicate my life to this monstrosity, and let alone "Put it in the closet, we'll take it out when she comes over," I would have to encase the damn thing in glass to try to prohibit it from shattering spontaneously.

It occurs to me that the three prime examples of bitchiness are three of the four women closest to me (the fourth being my daughter, who is too young and partakes of too much of my forthright nature ever to be a bitch). So I would, for a moment, speak like a member of the "helping professions," and suggest that people can't be bitchy to us unless we let them be close to us. This is a splendid theory and would hold water unless one had ever tried to complete a transaction in a New York bank.

I once spent about an hour in line at a New York bank waiting to make a deposit. When my turn finally came, I handed the teller my savings passbook and a check for twenty-five hundred dollars, meant for deposit. The teller credited the money to my passbook, then returned the passbook along with twenty-five hundred dollars in cash.

As I am a well-brought-up individual, my cupidity was inched out by my fear of being caught, and I said to the teller: "Excuse me ... ?" to which she responded, "You've had your turn, if you want another transaction, go to the back of the line." I stepped aside and meditated on how much sharper than *anything* it is to do business with a New York bank, and *again* my fear of capture came to the fore. I got in the somewhat shorter line which led to the bank officers. After about a half hour it came my turn, and I explained the situation to a vice president. She nodded, took the twenty-five hundred and began and *ended* her speech of thanks with the simple "Well, what are *you* waiting for?"

And speaking of the Capital of Bitchiness:

I was walking down the street on a beautiful New York day,

hurrying to a business meeting. I had on a sports coat as I thought I would comport myself in a deferential manner. I was not wearing a tie because I do not own a tie.

Passing Bendel's, I thought I would improve the few moments before my business meeting by buying a tie, so completing my "professional drag," and, in the very act of the transaction, becoming one with the mercantile society around me.

I went into the men's boutique section and smiled approvingly at the well-turned-out young woman in charge.

Ingenuously, I said, "Hi. I got dressed up for a business meeting. I put on a special outfit, and it occurs to me that I should have a tie. Which tie do you think I should choose to go with this outfit?" The young woman looked at me for a moment and responded, "Get a new outfit."

Yes, I admire it: the ability to spew those pungent periods right on the spur—the bile of a wasted life tempering the steel of a vicious disposition . . . for the world is full of cruelty, and how can we cease being cruel if we are *not* cruel?

Once in the midst of a particularly bad day I was having lunch at a crowded eatery. I was asked to share a table with a pretty woman in a proclaimedly unpleasant mood.

Being by profession, experience, and inclination suspicious and not a bit paranoid, I took her truculent silence personally. On arising to pay the check I nodded at my accidental table partner and said, "Nice chatting with you." She looked up and said, "My best friend died today," to which I responded, "Hey, Bitch, *I* didn't kill her. . . ." Laugh if you will, cry if you must, but I like to think, like bitches everywhere, that my quick and elegant rejoinder raised that woman from the morass of her legitimate personal problems, and enmired her in mine.

NOTES FOR A CATALOGUE
FOR RAYMOND SAUNDERS

My shoulder bag broke and I took it to the shoe repair
shop.
The cobbler looked at it and said that it would cost me ten
dollars to have the strap repaired. I protested this seemed
rather high.
He told me that it could not be fixed by machine and
would take at least an hour of hand-work.
All right, I said, when should I come back, next week?
No, he said, go get a cup of coffee, come back in ten or
fifteen minutes.
I had the bag in Louisiana, where I'd gone to meet an old
gunfighter.
I asked him if he'd like a cigar. No, he said, I only want
to know what's in the bag.
I saw that he thought the bag suspect, and explained that I
had my notebooks and pens in it. Next week, back East, I
realized he thought this *more* suspect. Today I see in the
New York *Times* that ultra-fashionable men have taken to
wearing skirts.

I always like to look at the title first. Like the rest I was
brought up saying that I had a five-year-old child at home
who could do as well; and also wondered, "Yes, but would
he show me he can adequately draw a horse?"
I always wanted to see the horse first. What does that
mean? Finally I have to tell myself it means that I am not
judging the art and not even judging the artist but am
judging myself.
Whence this idea that the purpose of painting is to allow
the viewer to exercise judgment?
People always ask me where I get my ideas. I always tell
them that I *think* of them. There seems to be a great confusion about the purpose of technique, and most of us, raised
in states which begin with a vowel, unconsciously agree
that the purpose of technique is to free the viewer from the
onerous responsibility of experiencing anything.
A well-drawn dog is better than a badly drawn lion.
Also we confuse "I like it" with "It is very realistic."
If we like it we say, "Yes, that's very true." And so our
judgment of techniques becomes a peremptory challenge
for that which we do not like.
Alfred Hitchcock. Doesn't that just capture the essence of
A. Hitchcock. "Yes, but it doesn't really *look* like that...
"Yes, but it's a play."
I once wrote a movie about Lawyers, who wrote in droves
to say that real lawyers don't behave that way. Someone
was guilty. "What in the world does this nonsense have to
do with *me* ... ?"
In a world we find terrifying, we ratify that which doesn't
threaten us.
Wishing things would go away.
It is all right for an orchid to look like female genitalia,
but may be objectionable for someone to call attention to
that similarity...

Why do fat adolescent girls have bandages on their calves?

How is it you always know when a salesperson is about to shortchange you?

Why is it that everyone knows that people tend to touch their nose when they lie but that we do not act on that information?

What does it mean that someone "has suffered enough," and why should we take their own word for it? Does it not seem that if someone has the gall to presume that this suggestion might forestall further grief that they have *not* suffered enough?

I have a friend who wanted to construct and market a down-filled Hawaiian shirt. *Does* this not render Tristan Tzara and the fur-lined teacup rather woosy?

Why is it that, stopped for a supposed traffic infraction, we can not *help* ourselves from saying, "What seems to be the trouble, Officer?" Would it make any difference if we said something else?"

Don Marquis said that the ultimate reconciliation of the Doctrine of Free Will and of Predestination was that we were free to do whatever we chose and whatever we chose to do would be wrong.

Judge says: Mr. X, can you account for your behavior?
Guy says: Judge, as a child I played the violin. The other
children shunned me, but I followed my star and I studied
every day.
A group of toughs called Legs O'Donnel and the Dead
Man's Lot gang put out word that if they ever caught me on
their turf that they would beat me silly.
So I stayed away from Dead Man's Lot.
One winter evening I was hurrying home. I'd studied late
and knew my mother would be worried, so I, timorously,
took the shortcut across Dead Man's Lot.
Halfway across I looked up and there was O'Donnel and
his gang. He said that they were going to beat me. I felt, if
I was to get a beating I would take it for that in which I
believed. So I took out my violin and played. I played as I
had never played before, and when I finished I looked up,
prepared to take my medicine.
And I found I was alone.
Many years later I was taking a cab through midtown and,
passing by the Artists' Entrance of Lincoln Center I saw
several men who looked familiar.
I asked the cabbie if he knew who those men were, and he
told me they were the Juilliard String Quartet.
I paid off the cab and stepped out on the sidewalk. I
stared at them.
The Juilliard String Quartet were no other than Legs
O'Donnel and the Dead Man's Lot gang.
It became clear to me that my playing for them on that
cold December night had turned them from a certain life of
crime and had inspired them to become the most accomplished string musicians in the world.
I drew nearer them and I saw recognition come into their
faces.
And they beat the shit out of me.

Rudolph Arnheim suggests we have difficulty perceiving true harmony in art as we are so seldom exposed to true harmony in our daily life.

We are becoming incapable of recognizing the harmonious and so begin to doubt that it exists.

What does it mean that we have eschewed the traditional tests of art, of conduct, of accomplishment in all forms?

Is it accidental that movies are worse than ever? and country songs—that last bastion of traditional free expression—increasingly make reference in their lyrics to the title of other country songs?

Every year the number of public places which do not broadcast music dwindles, and the quality of that music dwindles, too. We hear it in elevators, on airplanes, in lobbies, on the telephone. What is the purpose of this music? To delight? To express? It does neither. To soothe? I cannot find it soothing. I can only be enraged by it.

The question, it seems to me, is not what the Impresario thought he was selling when he put music in elevators, or what the Consumer thought he was buying.

The question, it seems to me, is what is the real meaning of the transaction.

And it seems to me that, in re: elevator music, we all—sellers, buyers, and victims, conspire to limit thought. Why?

Because those thoughts which might come in moments of repose are too frightening.

Our concerns with Corporate Takeovers, with Homosexuality, and Nuclear Power, with the Dissolution of the Family—taken singly each of these topics seems both significant and insoluble. Taken conjointly they seem to me to indicate a sort of social elevator music—a concern with the symptomatic rather than with the substantive.

I think these issues are a screen which prevents us from looking at ourselves.

We accept the degeneration which seems to be the order of the day ... in our health, in our social institutions, in our environment, in the World Situation.

Our poetry does not rhyme, our doctors cannot cure, our politicians cannot represent, our artists cannot explain.

It seems to me obvious that we are in line for a great and fast-approaching catastrophe of some sort and that nothing will avert it; that these symptoms are unimportant in themselves and are only the inescapable forewarnings of that which is to come.

As a deeply diseased body seeks to throw off its imbalance through the skin, the glands, the digestive system, so these frightening financial, nuclear, sexual, geophysical declines are only healthy symptoms of a diseased world experimenting in an attempt to bring itself back to health.

A countryside suffused with hope peopled by animals and
schooled in thought had by the roadside one small tree
which said:
The queen saw her chance and she took the chance to quit
She packed her bags and fled
She lives in Southern France
A bear lies in her bed.
The rose inside the luggage she had brought is withered
She has tied the bags with rope
The rope is frayed
The windowsill is scarred where she has lowered it.

DECADENCE

A vogue or fashion is nothing other than the irresistible expression of a profound longing. This expression has the power to affect society-at-large because it is unconscious and symbolic.

A fashion may seem to be the creation of one mind or will, but that will must be ratified by many: the producers, the critics, the media—*by the popular mind acting as one*, in short. The power of fashion is the power of the collective unconscious ratifying a collectively held wish.

The popularity of disaster movies, for example, expresses a collective perception of a world threatened by irresistible and unforseen forces which *nevertheless are thwarted at the last moment*. Their thinly veiled symbolic meaning might be translated thus: We are innocent of wrongdoing. We are attacked by unforeseeable forces come to harm us. We are, thus, innocent even of negligence. Though those forces are insuperable, *chance* will come to our aid and we shall emerge victorious. "Our own innocence (or know-nothingism) is our own most powerful weapon; and there is no lesson to be learned from this nearly escaped disaster, as it could not have been foreseen and it could not happen again".

The popularity of slice-and-dice, young-girl-murdered-by-an-ax movies expresses a psychotic misogny—a hatred of women and a hatred of sex. They symbolize, and our ratification of them symbolizes what the ax murderer symbolizes: a wish to be castrated: to be relieved of the burden of sexuality.

We are in the midst of a vogue for the truly decadent in art—for that which is destructive rather than regenerative, self-referential rather than outward-looking, elitist rather than popular. This decadent art is elitist because it cannot stand on its merits as a work of personal creation. Instead it appeals to a prejudice or prediliction held mutually with the audience.

This appeal is political, and stems from the political urge, which is the urge to control the actions of others. It is in direct opposition to the artistic urge, which is to express oneself regardless of consequences. I cite "performance art," "women's writing," and, on the less-offensive end of the scale, "nonbooks"—"The———Handbook," etc.—which are not books at all, but badges proclaiming a position.

Plays which deal with the unassailable investigate nothing and express nothing save the desire to investigate nothing.

It is incontrovertible that deaf people are people, too; that homosexuals are people, too; that it is unfortunate to be deprived of a full happy life by illness or accident; that it is sobering to grow old.

These events, illness, homosexuality, accident, aging, birth defects, equally befall the Good and the Bad individual. They are not the result of conscious choice and so do not bear on the character of the individual. They are not the fit subject of drama, as they do not deal with the human capacity for choice. Rather than uniting the audience in a universal experience, they are invidious. They split the audience into two camps: those who like the play and those who hate homosexuals (deaf people, old people, paraplegics, etc.).

Fashion in clothing is also the expression of a wish. It is the wish to co-opt the experience—the tragedy, the joy, the mobility—of that group being emulated. Military garments express the desire to be regimented; miniskirts expressed the wish to be without responsibility—to be considered as infants; the current punk fashion, in its comment on the fifties, is an indictment of the aridity of our parents' era.

In both the haute couture and street fashion we see the torn, the ragged, the baggy, the drab.

In musical videos, time and time again, battered children move jerkily, stare bleakly, standing in scenes of rubble. The videos portray a fantasy of autism. They stage our view of ourselves as abused children—abandoned, beaten, so imbued with rage that we are incapable of movement, as if the slightest movement would unleash an anger so uncontrollable that it would destroy us, those around us, and the world. This fantasy of autism masks overpowering anger, as does our acceptance and ratification of the nonbook, the nonplay, the photorealist painting.

And so art, the social purpose of which is to *create*, has been pressed into service as a *censor*, whose purpose is to *control*. We are left with this spectrum of expression: the Radical, which seeks to destroy (blank canvases, graffiti art); the Liberal, which seeks to reform (plays, books, films about homosexuality, feminism—works about *conditions* rather than about *character*); the Conservative, which seeks to lull, to distract, to sentimentalize (E.T., the Muppets); the Fascist, which seeks to control and manipulate (Walt Disney World, Up with People).

This spectrum of our National Mentality, this one-party system, is not a conspiracy, but a *trend*. The trend expresses our deep wish to deny. The trend silences ferment, stills inquiry, and, at no point, allows the purpose of true art, the purpose of which is to *create*.

The absence of the urge to create is decadence.

A FAMILY VACATION

My people have always been anxious about traveling. I think this dates back to the Babylonian Exile. In any case, when I was growing up, the smallest move was attended by fear, puttering, and various manifestations of nerves. My father and mother would fight, we would invariably get lost, we would miss meals, bedtimes, and destinations entirely.

My parents' fears took many convenient forms: fear of polio, of contamination from drinking fountains, of drowning from swimming too close on the heels of eating . . . all of these were just handy guises for the severest xenophobia, which I saw all around me as a child, in my home and my friends' homes.

Looking back, the fear of the strange that I saw around me is understandable, and I am only half kidding in referring to it as a cultural trait. My parents and the parents of my friends were one short generation removed from The Pale of Settlement in Russo-Poland; and to *their* parents the shortest trip away from home offered real possibilities of real trouble: difficulty of obtaining food acceptable to their religious laws, of confusion as to the local customs, of persecution and murder itself.

So this was the jolly burden which my parents inherited

from their parents and passed down to me; and seventy years removed from the Cossacks I was still unable to take a vacation.

On our honeymoon, my wife and I went to Paris and I spent two days curled up on the bed. Yes, you will say, correctly, that probably had something to do with getting married—but isn't that a journey of a sort as well?

The above specious observation to the contrary notwithstanding, in eight years of marriage, and based on our informative experiences on the honeymoon, we have not really had a vacation.

But this year it occurred to both of us that we were not going to live forever, that our daughter was not forever going to stay a fascinating, loving, three-year-old, and that on our respective deathbeds we were going to be unlikely to say, "I'm glad I advanced my career in 1986."

So my wife, speaking not for herself, but for the Group, signed us up to take a vacation. A model husband, I, of course, agreed and congratulated her on her decision, knowing that as the time came to leave, I could find some pull of work that kept me at home, or at the very best, feign sickness, and failing that, I could actually *become* sick.

The last being a tactic I'd employed before and to advantage: "*You* girls go away, don't worry about me, go and refresh yourselves," and then they'd go, and I could stretch out over the whole bed and smoke cigars in the living room.

But this time it was not to be. And, as the day set for departure drew near, I told my wife that I was heartbroken, but I could not accompany them; to which she replied that she had checked my datebook, and I had nothing scheduled for the week in question save a haircut appointment, which she had canceled for me; and that she had already told the kid how Daddy was going to come down for a week and "not work."

Well, I fought a holding action on the rectitude of her having unilaterally canceled my haircut appointment, and on the collateral issue of my well-known inability to enjoy myself when my hair is too long. To which arguments my wife responded, "Tough," and off we went to fun and frolic in the Caribbean surf.

On the way to the airport, the cabbie asked us why we were going to vacation on an island which was currently being decimated by a hurricane. I thought, Aha! The cavalry arrives. But my wife said, "We're going down there to find out, and if it has not passed we'll just come home, and that's what we're going to do." We prepared to get on the plane.

I explained to my wife that on the plane going down I was going to have to do research, and she said, "Fine." My research consisted of reading the galleys of a detective novel someone wanted to make into a movie, and my enjoyment of it would have been increased if she had resisted, but she did not. So I struggled through the book. My daughter watched *Romancing the Stone*, and my wife colored in the kid's coloring book for three and a half hours.

At the island we found that the hurricane had indeed passed, so I scowled and we went off to our hotel. We got to the hotel, and I braced for what the Semitic Traveler will of course recognize as the interlude of: I am here, I am paying good money, everything is wrong. Change everything immediately and make it different or I am going to die.

The bellman put the bags in the room, I open the doors to the patio beyond which was the sand beach and the Caribbean, and a football landed with a huge "plop" in the water outside.

Fine, I thought, here I'm paying good money for some peace and quiet, and some overly American jock who can't leave home without his props is going to ruin my vacation.

Then as I watched, the football opened its wings and revealed itself to be a pelican which had just dived for a fish.

Okay, I thought, I'll try. And I did try. I changed into my suit and sat on the beach. I thought about Somerset Maugham and his sea stories. I thought about Joseph Conrad. I picked up a seashell and thought how very Victorian it looked, and wondered at the Multiplicity of Nature.

The sun went down, we put the baby to bed, and my wife and I went to dinner. We sat in a beautiful restaurant, hanging out on a cliff over the beach. There was a "popping" sound below, like far-off fireworks. I looked and saw the sound was made by the undertow, dragging the stones behind it. I said, "The stones on the beach being dragged sound like far-off fireworks." My wife said nothing. I said, "It occurs to me that the teaching of literature is completely *wrong*. Now: here we have a lovely simile—but the point is not the *simile* ... the point is not the writer's knack at making a *comparison*— the point is the *stone!*"

My wife said, "Why don't you take a vacation?"

Well, I had another drink, then I had *another* drink, then we went back to our room and we fell asleep, and I slept for eighteen hours on each of the next two days, and on the third day I wasn't thinking about Joseph Conrad anymore.

My daughter asked me to come out and make "flour," and rather than responding "Just a minute" I went out and made flour. Making flour consisted of pouring sand into a palm leaf, and I was surprised to find it just as enjoyable as (and certainly more productive than) a business lunch at the Russian Tea Room.

The punch line was that we had a grand old time. We swam and went waterskiing, we had breakfast on the patio. The baby went naked on the beach for a week with a strand of beads around her neck, and her hair got bleached and streaked.

Some good friends were vacationing on a neighboring island, and they came over for a day and we all got drunk and went skinny-dipping in the moonlight; my daughter and I bounded on a trampoline a couple of hours every day; and all in all, it was the trip of a lifetime.

I thought: we are Urban people, and the Urban solution to most any problem is to do more: to find something new to eat in order to lose weight; to add a sound in order to relax; to upgrade your living arrangements in order to be comfortable; to buy more, to eat more, to do more business. Here, on the island, we had nothing to do. Everything had been taken away but the purely natural.

We got tired as the sun went down, and active when it rose; we were treated to the rhythm of the surf all day; the heat and the salt renewed our bodies.

We found that rather than achieving peace by the addition of a *new idea* (quality time, marital togetherness, responsibility), we naturally removed the noise and distractions of a too-busy life, and so had *no need* of a new idea. We found that a more basic idea sufficed: the unity of the family.

I did leave the island two days earlier than they, as I had to be in Los Angeles on business. As I got on the plane, I harbored a small secret joy at my forthcoming return to the addiction of busy life: I would have meetings and talk on the phone and lounge across the bed and smoke cigars in the hotel room.

I waved from the plane window and put my writer hat back on, and several thoughts occurred to me. The first was of Thorstein Veblen, who said that nobody traveling on a business trip would ever have been missed if he did not arrive. And I said to myself, you know, that's true.

And I thought Hippocrates, and his hospital on the island of Cos, where the sick were treated to a peaceful view, and warm winds, and the regenerative rhythm of the surf—to a place where man could be healed because the natural order was allowed to reassert itself; and I missed my family, and was very grateful for the week that we spent with each other on the beach.

SEMANTIC CHICKENS

In our motion-picture theaters big black scary monsters interfere with white starlets.

Huge and persistent sharks devour tugboats.

Things burn, crumble, and/or are inundated with unpleasant amounts of water.

These are our world-destruction dreams. There is, in our dream life, no certainty. We objectify our insecurity and self-loathing in the form of outside forces endeavoring to punish us.

They may not know what we have done, but *we* do.

We turn on our television and we see one show after another glorifying our law-enforcement agencies.

We are an open book.

We propitiate those forces we elect to stave off, those who would take our electric ranges from out of our kitchenette.

We pay homage to the medical profession, glorifying them as superbeings capable of not only *understanding* the diseases of both the sick and worried, but of *caring* about them.

Surely we must be safe from terrors both of corporeal and social malefactors. The Cop on the Beat and the Doc in the ER protect us. Zeus is great.

Our tenuous monotheism disappears in the face of our great

insecurities, and we live once again overtly in an animistic universe surrounded by superbeings.

There is no surety. What is the use of discrimination in a world where anything can happen?

Our magazines are full of photographs of naked men and women. Our pulp literature is the same tale told over and over again: the world is ending, only one man or woman (a spy, or a soldier, or a news reporter, or an ordinary citizen) possesses the ability to save it.

They tromp through the book and get laid and get hit on the head and save the world at the end and then they go home.

What are we telling ourselves through this popular culture?

Why are we, as a nation, and in the persons and through the abilities of our artists, constantly ending the world?

This is my question. Certainly, it indicates a great abiding and inchoate anger.

As Mr. Chayefsky told us so brilliantly in *Network*, we would like to say, "We are mad as hell, and we aren't going to take it anymore."

But we are going to take it, and we do take it, and we have a great amount of trouble expressing it because we don't trust words. Our anger is so great we can only blurt and stammer. Our semantic chickens have come to roost.

We have bought so many things labeled *improved* which were only repackaged that we no longer believe that something *may*, in fact, be improved.

We have watched our constitutional government suborned by petty, hateful men and women sworn to obey the law, and we have heard them characterize their crimes as actions taken in the public interest. Consequently we have come to doubt that it is *possible* to act in the public interest.

My generation grew up in a time when constant vicious aggression publicly avowed came to be the norm of our foreign policy. We had changed the name of the Department of War to the Department of Defense, and went about making war continually and calling it defense until today we doubt if there *is* such a thing as defense, or if, in fact, the real meaning of defense is not "aggression."

We have come to accept all sorts of semantic inversions, just as George Orwell told us we would.

And now, overcome by information, decimated by anger and feeling completely impotent, we feel unequipped to do other than submit to whatever next atrocity chooses to take stage, be it another psychopathic public official or a giant ape.

But I wonder if this is necessary. I wonder how we can eliminate the boogeyperson from beneath the bed.

We are so ruled by magic. We have ceased to believe in logic. The cause to which we attribute so many effects is, thinly masked, our own inadequacy.

We take refuge in mumbo jumbo, in the Snake Oil of the Seventies, in escapism.

But the people must have what they want. If the people want trash, they will *have* trash. Trash at the movies, trash on stage, trash in the bookstore, trash in Office, trash at the supermarkets.

What can we do to overcome this habit of saying, in effect, things are not what they seem to be, but what we are told that they are?

A good first step might be to turn off the television sets.

(On a more serious note, after the catyclysm, be it giant ape or flash flood or tongue of newt or whatever, there will be no more television, neither will there—for a while—be a motion-picture "industry." There will be only human beings and the human urge to dramatize. There will be theater, and those who will be in the "know" will be those who have sharpened their sensibilities through preholocaust attendance, so get out more.)

Another good idea would be to go to the theater when you feel the need of diversion. The theater, in the main, uses live personnel, and one can go backstage afterward and tell the

actors and actresses and the director and writer, if they are
around, that what you saw did not make sense, and recom-
mend that they fix it.

For just as the purpose of the motion picture is the gradual
revelation of the human genitalia, and the purpose of television is the support of several manufactories of small arms
in Connecticut, just so the purpose of the theater is the making
of sense.

To become very parochial, the purpose of the theater, as
Stanislavsky said, is to bring to light the life of the human
soul; and the theater, essentially and even today, possesses
this potential. Alone among community institutions the theater possesses the power to differentiate between truth and
garbage. We do not always acquit ourselves of our responsibility to the limits of our power, but we have the power.
There are live people on stage and live people in the audience,
and if the words and the actions do not come out even,
everybody knows it—we may not always admit it, but we
always know it. We have no helicopter shots, we have no
EKGs, we have no press secretaries. We do not have to sell
soap.

Perhaps if we went to the theater more we might learn to
regain our faith in words. If we went and watched and listened
and made some demands.

My premise is that things do mean things; that there is a
way things *are* irrespective of the way we *say* things are, and
if there isn't, we might as well act as if there were. "And
that's how it is on this bitch of an earth."

CHICAGO

Chicago's literary history truly begins around the turn of the century with Alderman Bathhouse John Coughlin, coruler (with Hinky Dink Kenna) of the First Ward, Chicago's Downtown.

From Coughlin's "Ode to a Bathtub":

> *Some find enjoyment in travel, others in*
> *Kodaking views.*
> *Some take to automobiling in order themselves*
> *to amuse.*
> *But for me there is only one pleasure, although*
> *you can call me a dub—*
> *There's nothing to my mind can equal a plunge*
> *in a porcelain tub.*

Fifty years later the ward found another champion in Richard J. Daley—he is gone but he will never be forgotten—the man who said, "The police of the City of Chicago are not there to create disorder, but to preserve the existing disorder." Let it also be noted that a previous mayor, Big Bill Thompson, once threatened to punch the King of England in the nose, an un-Chicagoan sentiment, as we have always been kind to visitors.

Hedda Gabler had its world premiere in Chicago, as Ibsen couldn't get anybody to produce it at home. Ten blocks away and twenty years later Al Capone ruled the city from his headquarters in the Lexington Hotel.

J. J. Johnston, a Chicago actor, told me Al's wife was an Italian girl, and that she was never accepted by her husband's family until the day of his funeral. Overcome by grief she stood by the grave and proclaimed, "Al created an empire on earth, and he will build another one in heaven." After which she was accepted into the fold.

Dreiser worked on Wabash Avenue downtown, and he used to eat at the Berghof Restaurant. Every time we went from the Goodman Theater over to the Berghof for lunch, I wondered if this was the restaurant Hurstwood was managing when he met Sister Carrie. And when we rehearsed plays in the Fine Arts Building on Michigan Avenue, I wondered if the woman practicing *sol-fe* could have run into Lucy Gayheart (or at least Willa Cather) in the old iron elevator.

(The woman was there when I started studying piano in 1951, and she was there when we were rehearsing *Native Son* in 1980. I see no reason she shouldn't have been there trying to hit that same goddamned note in 1905.)

We have some strange local mythology.

Nobody makes gangster jokes or thinks of the city as particularly violent (which it isn't). Yet we do make police jokes and take pride in considering the force *haimishly* corrupt (which it isn't). And we take *great* pride in our excellent fire department.

Robert Quinn, fire commissioner till just lately, was an old friend and crony of Mayor Daley. Their association went back to the days of the Hamburger Athletic Club in Bridgeport— Chicago's equivalent to having been there in the Oriente Mountains. So Quinn was fire commissioner forever.

In 1978 there was a furor because Quinn, rather than purchasing efficient, van-type paramedic ambulances, was still contracting for the old-fashioned low-slung Cadillacs. Interviewed on television news, he said, "I think when the people of the City of Chicago do go, they want to go in *style*." This caused something of a commotion, and the next night Quinn called a news conference to defend himself and explained, "What I *meant* was the People of Chicago, when they *go*, they want to go in *style*."

God bless our journalists. Carl Sandburg once wrote film reviews for the *Daily News* (Chicago's greatest newspaper— eight years now demised, and may it rest forever in peace and in our memories). Dreiser was a drama critic in town; Hecht and MacArthur worked for City News Service; Nelson Algren was a reporter, as was Vachel Lindsay, our finest poet Midwesterner.

Lindsay was writing of Bryan's campaign visit to Springfield, Illinois, but he might as well have been writing of Chicago:

> She wore in her hair a brave prairie rose.
> Her Gold friends cut her, for that was not
>   the pose.
> No Gibson Girl would wear it in that fresh
>   way.
> But we were fairy Democrats, and this was
>   our day.

In our beloved Windville we curse the cold and revel in being the most senseless spot in North America to spend the winter in. But the air feels new, and all things still seem possible, as they did to Willa Cather and Sherwood Anderson and Willard Motley and Hemingway and Frank Norris and Saul Bellow and all the other Chicago writers who—when speaking of Home—finally wrote the same story. It was and is a story of possibility, because the idea in the air is that the West is beginning, and that life is capable of being both understood and enjoyed.

Those writers exhorted us, as did their philosophical confrere Alderman Hinky Dink Kenna—Bathhouse John's partner in crime:

"Whatever the endeavor, make of it a lollapalooza."

With thanks to Chicago historians Mark Jacobs and Kenan Heise.

ON PAUL ICKOVIC'S
PHOTOGRAPHS

I have always felt that people look on me as an outcast—that the simple request for a cup of coffee elicits a slight tightening around the eyes.

I have always felt like an outsider; and I am sure that the suspicion that I perceive is the suspicion that I provoke by my great longing to *belong*.

I would like to live a life free of constant self-examination— a life which may be ruled by the processes of guilt, remorse, hope, and anxiety, but one in which those processes them- selves are not foremost in the mind.

I would like to belong to a world dedicated to creating, preserving, achieving, or simply getting by. But the world of the outsider, in which I have chosen to live, and in which I have trained myself to live, is based on none of those things. It is based on observation.

The habit of constant *acute* awareness can be seen in an- imals with no recourse, with no option to fight, with no margin for error. It is the habit of one completely dependent on the vagaries and good will of his environment. It is the habit of the young child. Historically, it is the habit of the Jew.

As the children of immigrant Jews, we are spurred in our need to observe by the memory of old humiliations, of old indignities. We are spurred by the learned and enforced pleasures of isolation and reflection.

Trained to live by our wit, to live on margin—trained not to assimilate, we have found useless the virtues of compromise with our environment. And so our lives are a fierce attempt to find an aspect of the world that is not open to interpretation.

True to our past, we live and work with an inherited, observed, and accepted vision of personal futility, and of the beauty of the world.

A PLAYWRIGHT
IN HOLLYWOOD

I am a playwright, which is to say that what I have done with most of my time for most of my adult life is sit by myself, talk to myself, and write the conversation down.

This year I was hired to write a screenplay, and what had been—for better and worse—the most private of occupations became a collaborative endeavor.

I have never been much good as a team player or employee, and it was difficult for me to adjust to a situation where "because I say so" was insufficient explanation.

When you write for the stage you retain the copyright. The work is *yours* and no one can change a word without your permission. When you write for the screen you are a *laborer* hired to turn out a product, and that product can be altered at the whim of those who employ you.

When the meaning of the script is unclear in the theater, the actors and director usually assume that the author knew what he or she was doing, and they reapply themselves to understanding the script.

In the movies if the meaning and the worth of the script is not immediately obvious, everyone assumes the writer has failed.

That was the hard part of working in the movies; and if you have ever tried to explain why a joke you have just told actually *is* funny you know what I'm talking about.

One of the good things, on the other hand, about a year spent as an employee is that I received a lesson in consistency.

Most playwrights are acquainted with the basic rules of dramaturgy, and most of us—from time to time—cheat.

If the action of a character in one scene, for example, is to FLEE THE COUNTRY, we know that a good way to start would be by having him LEAVE THE ROOM. But most of us are loath to eliminate the moving "Death of my Kitten" speech the hero utters on his exit.

The necessary progression is:

TANIA   Franz, the Army of the Reds is in the Village Square, and you must leave.

FRANZ   See you in Bucharest. (*He exits*)

But we lie to ourselves, hoping that no one will notice the interruption of the action, and the scene is written:

TANIA   Franz, the Army of the Reds is in the Village Square, and you must leave.

FRANZ   Leave? Leave? How *many* ways there are to leave! When I was young I had a kitten ... (*etc.*)

"Yes," we say, "it's not consistent, but it sure is pretty. Why should I be bound by the rules of dramaturgy when no one knows them but me, and *my* understanding of them is by no means perfect?"

The rule in question here is Aristotle's notion of unity of action: in effect, that the play should be about only one thing, and that that thing should be *what the hero is trying to get*.

Unstinting application of this rule makes great plays because the only thing we, as audience, care about in the theater is WHAT HAPPENS NEXT?

All of us writers know this but few of us do it.

We don't do it because it is too difficult.

It is much easier to write great dialogue (which is a talent and not really very much of an exertion) than to write great plots. So we playwrights do the next best thing to writing great plots: we write *bad* plots. And then we fill up the empty spaces with verbiage. Or we assign interesting attributes to the characters so that the audience will care about them. (In the thirties a popular attribute was Great Wealth. In the fifties it was Lower-Class Background. In the seventies and the eighties it was Physical Handicap or Deformity.)

These attributes are super, but the only thing we want to know when our friends come back from the theater is, "What's it about?" We do not ask, "Are there heartwarming or compelling types involved who make me cry?"

Working in the movies taught me (for the moment, anyway) *to stick to the plot and not to cheat.*

Now we Americans have always considered Hollywood, at best, a sinkhole of depraved venality. And, of course, it is. It is not a Protective Monastery of Aesthetic Truth. It is a place where everything is incredibly expensive.

The movie is costing $100,000 a day to film. So it's not too bright to write a beautiful scene which impedes the plot, as, when the film is being cut and the editor has to get the turkey down from two hours fifteen minutes to two hours flat, the beautiful scene that impedes the plot is going to fall on the floor, and the writer has just wasted $100,000.

Hollywood's interest in economy took me back to early days in the theater.

When we put on plays in garages and in church basements everything used in the show was borrowed, stolen, or, as a last resort, purchased out of the cabdriving or waitressing wages of the company members.

This healthy relationship to financial necessity made for good theater because only that was put upon the stage which was unquestionably essential to the production.

Another instructive aspect of financial necessity which I rediscovered in the movies was an abiding concern for the audience.

In garage theater if you aren't funny they *don't come.*

This principle does not seem to be in force on Broadway, but it does apparently operate in the movies.

In an attempt to get the audience to buy their popcorn *before* the show, Bob Rafelson (*Postman*'s director and my sponsor in Hollywood) quizzed me about my screenplay relentlessly, and what he asked was this: *can it be better?*

When people have been calling you an Artist for a number of years your personal acquaintance with this question can fall into desuetude.

My work in a collaborative situation where I could not say "It's perfect. Act it" was a healthy tonic.

It reassured me about my ability to solve problems, and also about my ability to get along with people. The film's production people are pleased with themselves—not only do they have a good script, but they took a chance to get it; they have made a "discovery."

So that is my success story: someone felt it would be more rewarding to teach an artist a new technique than to attempt to induce a hack to be interesting, and everybody went home happy.

There is a *vast* amount of talent in this country's theater—in the small theaters of Chicago, Boston, New York, Louisville, and Seattle, especially. Theatrical artists in these and other cities are working. They are acting, designing, directing, and writing plays constantly. Because they live in an atmosphere fairly free of commercial pressure, they have no need either to withhold their skills from the marketplace to drive up the price, or to pander to mercantile aesthetics; so they are developing their skills, their point of view, and their talent.

Traditionally the movie industry has developed this talent by demonstrating to it how much better a Mercedes handles than a Chevy.

Collaborating with, rather than exploiting, this talent would make our Friday nights at the movies a lot more diverting.

It wouldn't be that difficult to do. It wouldn't even call for altruism on the part of the producers—just a little creative venality.

I have, personally, profited in several ways from my sojourn in Hollywood. I am going back to work on a new play with, I admit, a slight residual attitude of "Who *knew*? We all thought they were summer camps"; and I look forward to doing another movie.

OSCARS

We live in a world ruined by Reason.

If you take the faith out of Religion, you have a wasted Sunday morning. If you take the belief out of Law, all you have is litigation. And if you take the Ritual out of celebration, all you have is Presidents' Day.

Presidents' Day is a bastard amalgamation of the birthdays of George Washington and Abe Lincoln. Where once we had two distinct and spontaneously created national rituals, all we have is an extra day of leisure.

Each of these two presidential celebrations arose for a reason. One celebrated our own espousal of the virtues of dull honesty; one mourned the passing of a great soul.

But no paper cutout silhouettes are made for Presidents' Day, and no addresses are memorized and delivered, and no more is the bizarre story of the cherry tree retold. Reason has been applied and our Rich Uncle has awarded us another day off in the interest of increased productivity.

We do not arise from Presidents' Day refreshed; and we do not ask, as we ask at Passover, "Why is this night different from all other nights?" It isn't.

If you apply Reason to the Wake you might say, "Why

bother, he's dead *anyway*." But the naturally evolved use of Abe Lincoln's birthday was a reminder that there are qualities which we may strive to emulate which are both excellent and lovely. And now the celebration of Abe's birthday is no more.

As we have lost our barbershops and pool halls, our cousins clubs and fraternal organizations, so we have forsworn our rejuvenating rituals.

Only two legitimate national holidays remain. By "legitimate" holidays, I mean this: holidays with a specific, naturally evolved meaning, the celebration of which we find refreshing and correct, and in the celebration of which we, as a People, are united. Those holidays are the Super Bowl and the Academy Awards.

The Super Bowl, it seems to me, is a celebration of our national love of invidious comparison. We Americans love to find out if A is better than B, for—having located them on the Great Chain of Being—we are permitted to find points of goodness in both. To show fealty to the one and compassion to the other.

Having come the long way around the barn: what of the Oscars? I have enjoyed, looked forward to, and watched them for over thirty years. I have participated in them twice: once as a nominee, and once as backstage wife. In all capacities, I have found them fascinating and refreshing—different, distinct, different from all other days, delineating a set period— a true ritual whose meaning and forms have arisen from a mutual cultural necessity.

It is the physical and emotional exigencies of a ritual which reveal—much more than the verbal formula—the ritual's true meaning.

It is not written, but it is generally understood that the groom is supposed to be nervous and to wonder if he has lost the ring. He is buoyed up by the calm of the best man, who *himself* is somewhat anxious lest he lose the ring. So, as the close male friendship is partially dissolved in favor of marriage, the best man is consoled by being allowed both to share in the anxiety of his friend and to stand superior to his friend's display of emotion. The ritual eases parting through affirmation of the close tie and reassurance that the best man's life will continue in spite of his loss.

At the Oscars, we participants anxiously wonder: have I given the Academy the correct hotel address to which to deliver the tickets? Will they arrive in time? Should I put them in the safe? Will they be stolen? Do I really want another carafe of fresh orange juice, or am I just ordering it because the studio is paying for it and I want to punish them for subjecting me to this ordeal?

In the limousine, we cannot fathom why in the world we have left the hotel so early and what we will do with the extra time. As we approach the Pavillion, we wonder if we can possibly push through the traffic and arrive at all.

We find ourselves making stupid, predictable, and conventional remarks to those around us; *especially* to those in authority. And, childlike, we have broadened our definition of authority to include anyone who controls or directs us at the present moment: the limousine chauffeur, the desk clerk, the ticket taker. Reason has been suspended and we have regressed. We are no longer self-determined individuals, we have become children. In spite of ourselves, Ritual has evolved and enveloped us. We are once again part of the Tribe.

What do the Oscars mean? On some reflection, I think they mean this: they are a celebration of the power of the will of the people.

The Oscars demonstrate the will of the people to control and judge those they have elected to stand above them (much, perhaps, as in bygone days, an election celebrated the same).

The constituency of the moviemaker is the Entire Country. Everyone goes to the movies, and when we purchase a ticket, we make a sacrifice—a token but nonetheless real gesture of subservience. We make this gesture again in accepting the Movie Greats' enjoyment of their own prerogatives. When we read of their loves, their incomes, their foibles, their crimes, we shrug and smile, and, in so doing, we commit an act of subservience—we cede to others the ability to transgress the norms we have set up for ourselves.

At the Oscar ceremony, we, as people, compel those we have permitted into a privileged class to stand alone and hear the verdict. We, for one night, strip them of their privileges. And, just as in any court, the verdict itself is less important to the community than the power to summon. Just as at a court of law, the accused (the Oscar nominees) are compelled to hold themselves in a state of anxiety, nervous anticipation, and fear, and suffer the verdict passed on them.

Out in the audience, the Great, lured by the offer of a final laurel, hold themselves in fear of the unknown and are re-duced to uttering magic incantations, to wit: "It's an honor just to be nominated"; "I knew I was going to lose"; "Oh, why did I prepare a speech? I know that's going to blow it for me," etc.

We, the American public convened as a tribe, see the faces of these muttering nominees. And we see that they are finally just mortal folks who must bear their losses stoically and be graceful in victory—just like us. We force the Great—just as they forced Caesar— to sue the Crown, and we see that, by Jove, they *do* sue for it. How about that?

The Oscars are a kind of Purim. We, at home—no less than the gawkers behind the police barricades—are there to make fun of the Rabbi: "Oh, God, did you see her dress?..." "I heard he's gay...." "See how nervous he is...." "His movie was a bust and he's death at the box office...." "Why is she nervous? Doesn't she know she's never going to win?" We are united as a community in that most satisfying and unifying of social activities—gossip—the purpose of which is to define social norms. And, just as in another time we might have met around the cracker barrel, we are meeting around the TV to talk about them folks who live up on the hill. The Oscars are rather a beautiful ritual, I think. They celebrate both secrecy—devotion to tradition, and surprise—the healthy fear of God.

What would the Oscars be without the presence of the two men from Price Waterhouse? Every year their office as protectors of the faith erodes, and the traditional formula of the reading of the rules for balloting is made fun of. But, more important than the fact that it is mocked, is the fact that it is still there. The Oscars would not be quite right without Price Waterhouse. Why? Because those two ritualistically dumpy men assure us that—in spite of the vast rewards to be gained by irregularity—our interests as a people are being protected. There still may be a surprise winner, God and the Devil still exist.

The ritualistically awful quality of the entertainment seems to proclaim this: that the true purpose of the event is not the celebration of excellence, but the celebration of ordeal.

The traditional confusion, sarcasm, or stupidity of the Presenters is a disclaimer on their part of participation in the ordeal at hand ("Don't confuse me with tonight's potential victims. I am so far from their anxiety—as you see—that I don't even know what's going on here"). The presenters—lured by the offer of mass publicity—are also there to witness the power of the pageant and to educate themselves in the correct behavior of the victims.

When one is nominated for but passed over by the Academy Awards, one is told this: "It's a great honor just to be nominated." And, of course, it is, for it means that one has been tapped out as powerful, and, as such, elected to make a pledge to the people.

When the winner is revealed, he is expected to reveal himself—to be reduced to humility or confusion by the great honor done him. And, having left the podium, the winner is expected to display either giddy abandon or discernible ambition. Either one will do. Much as, among the four or five nominees, anyone will do.

And any winner will do. We'll cheer Our Side if they win, and we'll curse if we lose, they're both equally enjoyable. Also enjoyable is this: The Oscars are a final verdict. They have an end, and—much as Lent does—they mark the end of a period which now will begin anew. What a lovely ceremony, and how flattering that society has elected Motion Picture Art to be the backdrop for it.

The wake probably began as an attempt to capture a few last moments with the spirit of the departed. A more important function emerged—the comfort of the widow. This function is so important, so powerful (for it blesseth him that gives and him that takes) that it must be masked. Just so, the Oscars began as an in-house ceremony of appreciation. They have evolved into The Big Bar Mitzvah. Like that more senior ceremony, they command a demonstration of subservience to the will of the Tribe.

This once-a-year ritual obeisance to tribal will is as important for those inside the movie industry as it is for those outside.

Just as on that day in England, when the masters and the staff change clothes, it reminds the masters that there *is* a limit, and that God has not damned them for omnipotent power. On that day, the masters get, for a moment, to live in that envied state of being "just folks."

The moviemakers are made to stand review on television; and then cleansed, held for a moment between one period and the next. Forgiven, shriven, if you will, they all tromp off to the Governors' Ball at the Beverly Hilton Hotel. There they eat chicken and dance with each other's wives. Much as they might at an automobile awards banquet in Detroit. They have served the people and now they are entitled to be refreshed.

If I were of a hortatory bent, I would suggest we put the gossip and philosophy back into the courts of law, Bert Parks back into the Miss America Pageant, and strike off Presidents' Day from our too-sad calendar.

But as Spengler reminds us, we may not have chosen to live in this unfortunate time, but nobody asked us. As it is, I am thankful for the Oscars. As an American, I thoroughly enjoy the ritual. As a sometimes-member of the film industry, I am proud that my group has been chosen to stand as acolytes.

POOL HALLS

The novel *The Hustler* is set in
a Chicago poolroom called "Benningtons," pool-shooting capital of the world.

The actual name of the Chicago poolroom was Bensinger's.
The Bensinger family owned Brunswick Corporation. Brunswick held, and perhaps still holds, the copyright on the word
"pool," which is a trademarked name for pocket billiards,
and I used to play pocket billiards at Bensinger's in Chicago.

The pool hall I played at was not quite the one immortalized
in the novel. A postwar cleanup of Chicago's Downtown Area
eradicated much of the demimonde living there, and the passing of the railroads took care of the rest.

When I was a habitué, Bensinger's had moved from Ran-
dolph Street up to the North Side, and its sign said that it
was called Clark and Diversey Billiards, but the clientele, of
course, still called it Bensinger's.

The pool hall opened, if memory serves, at eleven o'clock
in the morning. And that was a wonderful time to arrive,
especially in the summer, when Chicago was hot. You'd come
out of the glare and the concrete-trapped heat, down a long
flight of stairs, and there you were in this dark cavern.

In the cavern were forty pool tables, six three-cushion-billiard tables, snooker tables, a separate exhibition room, a bar, and a short-order kitchen. So there you are. It's eleven o'clock of a hot morning, you walk through the louvered doors and are greeted by Bob Siegel, who either did or did not own the place. Bob had been a postman, and remembered everybody's name that he had ever met. So if you'd been there every day since the Downtown Days, or if you'd been in once ten years ago, when you came by he greeted you by name, and he'd say "regular table?" and you'd say "yes," and he'd hand you the tray with the balls on it, and you'd say "I'm going on sixteen," or whatever table you were particularly enamored of in that period, and he'd nod, and you'd start off to your table.

Then—here comes the best part—you would say—over your shoulder—"would you send *John* over with a cup of *coffee*, please?" and Bob would say "sure thing." So you walk back to table sixteen or table seventeen far in the back of the hall. Everything is brown, the light is brown, the tables are brown, the oak benches are brown, the air is brown but it's cool. And you arrange your book, or your hat, or your newspaper on the bench next to your table, and you turn on the light over the table, and you spill the balls out of the tray and onto the table with a jerk of the wrists; when you do it right, they hardly bounce at all, and they don't hurt the surface. Then you kind of fling the tray under the table and you sit down on the bench.

Now the thing is if you're going to have a cigarette before your coffee comes, and, of course, you are, and so you light your Camel, or your Lucky, maybe the pack's crumpled, and maybe it's the last cigarette from last night. You light it and you're in the Perfect Place.

People are supposed to gamble here, people are supposed to drink here, people are supposed to spend their days here in pursuit of skill, cunning, comradeship, and money. No one is supposed to be pompous here, or intrusive, or boring; no one will be held unaccountable for the bets they make, or the way that they comport themselves. But if they choose, they can choose to be left alone.

Well, there I am getting high on my first cigarette, or however it felt, getting cool down in the basement. There's the click of a couple of guys shooting pool back near the entrance. John brings my cup of coffee, and I say "thank you." He asks me if I want breakfast, and I tell him "thank you, yes, a little later..."

Several years later, and in the last years of Mayor Daley's life, there was a pool hall called The Golden Eight Ball, down off Rush Street on Walton, and it had Muzak, and orange-yellow felt on the tables, and it was decorated. You could find businessmen there, and young couples on a fun date, and it lasted for a couple of years, and then it was gone.

Just as Bensinger's was gone. In the mid-seventies, the neighborhood got a tad too upscale, and all us warbabies needed somewhere to live, and so there went the neighborhood.

On Clark and Diversey where once an American could shoot pool for an hour in the summer and then dash across the street to the Parkway Cinema and catch a double feature at the before-twelve price of seventy-five cents (program changed thrice-weekly, hard to believe, but it's true), now there were candle stores, and restaurants with cunning names, and the beautiful 3,500-seat Century Movie Palace gutted to house a shopping mall.

Bensinger's moved again, down the street and up a flight of stairs over a record store. There were ten tables and Bob Siegel kept apologizing that they hadn't got the carpet in, so one had to stand on concrete all day long.

Bob, of course, never got the carpet in before the place got closed, a year or so later, and then there was nowhere to go.

Similarly in New York, on Eighth Avenue amid the girlie

peep shows, you could walk down two flights into McGirr's Pool Hall and there the same setup, minus the bar and grill; and people were selling dope and people were selling stolen merchandise and booking horses over the telephone and shooting a little pool into the bargain, and, around 1980, they closed that one down, too; they opened on Seventy-ninth and Broadway in New York, which currently is a Rug Warehouse. My question is where are the pool halls? And the answer is they're gone.

There is one on the main street in Gloucester, Massachusetts, and I went in there one day and tipped the guy five dollars to disconnect the video games for one hour so I could shoot pool in peace. After the hour was up, he was pressured from the teenagers and he wouldn't renew my deal, so I packed up and left.

There used to be a pool hall in the airport in Detroit, which I thought was the most civilized accoutrement I could imagine for an airport, and very advanced. It may still be there. And there was a pool hall downstate Illinois where they took a lot of money from me while I was waiting for a train to get me out of downstate Illinois one time.

But, basically, I think we have to say they're gone.

The point was not to play pool. One can do that, to a certain extent, in the Family Billiard Centers one sees stuck now and then in the Concrete Suburbs. And dads go there to have some sort of fun with their progeny. But the point of the pool hall was not fun. The point of the pool hall was the intersection of two American Loves: the Game of Skill and the Short Con.

The denizens of the pool hall came in to practice their skill, and the transients were those upon which the skill was practiced.

So you had to be near a transient neighborhood; you had to be in a neighborhood in transition; you had to be near the railroad.

Well, I guess that America is gone. We no longer revere

skill, and the short con of the pool hustle and the Murphy Man and the Fuller Brush Man. The short con, which flourished in a life lived on the street and among strangers, has been supplanted by the Big Con of a life with no excitement in it at all.

You see the clunky old elephant-legged pool tables from those old pool halls for sale from time to time, refinished, lovely leather pockets, beautiful new felt; and you might have a fantasy of taking them and housing them someplace, and that's what happened to the Country-at-Large: we turned America into a Den. Where could you be more wonderfully alone than in those old pool halls? You could sit there all day and no one would bother you except the occasional guy come over to say "shoot a game of eight-ball. Split the time?" and you'd say "no," thank God, and you could stay all day.

You could sit there and drink your coffee and go find the good House cue where you hid it up behind the ventilator (where you'd have to sort through the *other* House sticks that everyone *else* hid up behind the ventilator) and you'd shoot a little pool.

If you got hungry, you could raise your head and John would come over and you'd order breakfast and a *Daily News*, and maybe another pack of Camels.

Later you could amble to the bar, where they would have the Cubs (who played three blocks away) on the TV, and have a beer. Bob would call over "time off, Dave?" and you'd say "yeah, time off."

One night in the Exhibition Room, Sr. Juan Navarro, billed as Billiards Champion of the World, ran any number of straight-rail billiards, shot left-handed, made a billiard shooting *from one table to the next*. One night at the joint on Seventy-ninth Street me and a friend got lured from a nine-ball game where we had beat the local hustler, and he got us into the backroom and involved in a crap game where he cleaned us out with Shapes. One night I beat a guy in eight-ball at a bar, and he paid up and later followed me out into the night, until I turned around and looked at him, and I could see that he was just confused.

The best times were the days—the late mornings and the afternoons away from the world in a pool hall. "Let everything else revolve," you would think, "I've gone fishin'. I am nowhere to be found. I am nowhere. No one can find me here."

THINGS I HAVE LEARNED
PLAYING POKER ON THE HILL

In twenty years of playing poker, I have seen very few poor losers.

Poker is a game of skill and chance. Playing poker is also a masculine ritual, and, most times, losers feel either sufficiently chagrined or sufficiently reflective to retire, if not with grace, at least with alacrity.

I have seen many poor winners. Most are eventually brought back to reality. The game itself will reveal to them that they are the victim of an essential error: they have attributed their success to divine intervention.

The poor winner is celebrating either God's good sense in sending him down lucky cards, or God's wisdom in making him, the lucky winner, technically superior to the others at the table. In the first case, the cards will eventually begin to even out and the player will lose; in the second case, both the Deity and the players will tire of being patronized. The Deity will respond how he may, but the players will either drop out of the game or improve. In either case the poor winner will lose, and pride, once again, will go before a fall.

Speaking of luck: is there such a thing as luck? Yes. There is such a thing as luck. There is such a thing as a *run of luck*. This is an instructive insight I have gained from poker—

that all things have a rhythm, even the most seemingly in-animate of statistics.

Any mathematician will tell you that the cards at the poker table are distributed randomly, that we remember the re-markable and forget the mundane, and that "luck" is an illusion.

Any poker player knows—to the contrary—that there are phenomenal runs of luck which defy any mathematical ex-planation—there are periods in which one cannot catch a hand, and periods in which one cannot *not* catch a hand, and that there *is* such a thing as absolute premonition of cards: the rock-bottom *surety* of what will happen next. These things happen in contravention of scientific wisdom and common sense. The poker player learns that sometimes both science and common sense are wrong; that the bumblebee *can* fly; that, perhaps, one should never trust an expert; that there are more things in heaven and earth than are dreamt of by those with an academic bent.

It is comforting to know that luck exists, that there is a time to push your luck and a time to gracefully retire, that all roads have a turning.

What do you do when you are pushing your luck beyond its limits? You must behave like a good philosopher and ask what axiom you must infer that you are acting under. Having determined that, you ask if this axiom, in the long run, will leave you a winner. (You are drawing to a flush. You have a 1-in-4½ chance. The pot is offering you money odds of 5 to 1. It seems a close thing, but if you did it all day, you must receive a 10 percent return.)

If the axiom which you are acting under is not designed to make you money, you may find that your real objective at the game is something else: you may be trying to prove yourself beloved of God.

You then must ask yourself if—financially and emotion-ally—you can afford the potential rejection. For the first will certainly and the second will most probably ensue.

Poker is boring. If you sit down at the table to experience excitement, you will consciously and subconsciously do those things to make the game exciting; you will take long-odds chances and you will create emergencies. They will lose you money. If your aim, on the other hand, is to win money, you will watch the game and wait for the good cards, and play the odds-on chance, and, in the long run, you must be a winner. And when you do *not* win, you can still go home without mumbling, for, as Woodrow Wilson said: "I would rather lose in a cause which will eventually prevail than triumph in a cause doomed to failure." (I'll bet that most of you didn't even know he was a poker player.)

Playing poker you must treat each hand, as Epictetus says, as a visit to the Olympic Games, each hand offering you the chance to excel in your particular event—betting, checking, managing your money, observing the players, and, most often, waiting.

The poker players I admire most are indeed like that wise old owl who sat on the oak and who kept his mouth shut and his eye on the action.

As for observation, Confucius said man cannot hide himself—look what he smiles at, look what he frowns at. The inability to hide is especially true of men under pressure, which is to say, gamblers. This is another reason for stoic and correct play.

When you are proud of having made the correct decision (that is, the decision which, in the long run, *must* eventually make you a winner), you are inclined to look forward to the results of that decision with some degree of impassivity. When you are so resolved, you become less fearful and more calm. You are less interested in yourself and more naturally interested in the other players: now *they* begin to reveal themselves. Is their nervousness feigned? Is their hand made already? Are they bluffing? These elections are impossible to make when you are afraid, but become easier the more content you are with your own actions. And, yes, sometimes you lose, but differences of opinion make both horse races and religious intolerance, and if you don't like to take a sporting chance, you don't have to play poker.

Poker will also reveal to the frank observer something else of import—it will teach him about his own nature.

Many bad players will not improve because they cannot bear self-knowledge. Finally, they cannot bear the notion that everything they do is done for a reason. The bad player will not deign to determine what he thinks by watching what he does. To do so might, and frequently would, reveal a need to be abused (in calling what must be a superior hand); a need to be loved (in staying for "that one magic card"); a need to have Daddy relent (in trying to bluff out the obvious best hand); et cetera.

It is painful to observe this sort of thing about ourself. Many times we'd rather suffer on than fix it. It's not easy to face that, rather than playing cards in spite of our losses, we are playing cards because of them.

But poker is a game played among folks made equal by their money. Each player uses it to buy his time at the table, and, while there, is entitled to whatever kind and length of enjoyment that money will buy.

The pain of losing is diverting. So is the thrill of winning. Winning, however, is lonelier, as those you've taken money from are not likely to commiserate with you. Winning takes some getting used to.

Many of us, and most of us from time to time, try to escape a blunt fact which may not tally with our self-image. When we are depressed, we re-create the world around us to rationalize our mood. We are then likely to overlook or misinterpret happy circumstances. At the poker table, this can be expensive, for opportunity may knock, but it seldom nags. Which brings us to a crass thought many genteel players cannot grasp; poker is about money.

The ability of a poker player is judged solely by the difference between his stack when he sat down and his stack when he got up. The point is not to win the most hands, the point is not even to win in the most games. The point is to *win the most money*. This probably means playing less hands than the guy who has just come for the action; it means not giving your fellow players a break because you value their feelings; it means not giving some back at the end of the night because you feel embarrassed by winning; it means taking those steps and creating those habits of thought and action which, in the long run, must prevail.

The long run for me—to date—has been a period of twenty years.

One day in college I promoted myself from the dormitory game to the *big* poker game Up on the Hill in town.

After graduation I would, occasionally, come back to the area to visit. I told myself my visits were to renew friendships, to use the library, to see the leaves. But I was really coming back to play in the Hill game.

Last September one of the players pointed out that five of us at the table that night had been doing this for two decades.

As a group, we have all improved. Some of us have improved drastically. As the facts, the statistics, the tactics are known to all, and as we are men of equal intelligence, that improvement can be due to only one thing: to character, which, as I *finally* begin to improve a bit myself, I see that the game of poker is all about.

PART III

■

LIFE IN THE THEATER

EPITAPH FOR
TENNESSEE WILLIAMS

The theater is a beautiful life but a harsh business. Just as the price of gold represents the thousands of unproductive work-hours spent seeking it, artistic fame and remuneration—though awarded to the individual—represent society's debt to many.

That debt, though it may be paid quite gratefully, is rendered as a conditional trust rather than a perpetual freehold. It is subject to being withdrawn so that it may be awarded to another.

The pressure this creates to continually achieve makes playwriting a young man's game, for it is easily tolerated only by the inspired and naive—by those bursting with the joy of discovery and completely, unselfconsciously generous of that gift.

This generosity and superfluity of life compelled the public to Tennessee Williams's writing, and when his life and view of life became less immediately accessible, our gratitude was changed to distant reverence for a man whom we felt obliged— if we were to continue in our happy feelings toward him—to consider already dead.

His continued being and the fact of his later work disturbed our illusion; and we were embarrassed as our unease was hidden neither from ourselves nor from its subject, Tennessee. And we were piqued as he seemed neither to contest nor shun this attitude. He just kept writing.

We are a kind people living in a cruel time. We don't know how to show our love. This inability was the subject of his plays, the greatest dramatic poetry in the American language.

We thank him and we wish him, with love, the best we could have done and did not while he was alive. We wish him what he wished us: the peace that we all are seeking.

REGARDING
A LIFE IN THE THEATER

Thorstein Veblen wrote that typesetters were given to alcoholism in the 1880s because they belonged to a profession which was mobile and unstable.

They would switch jobs often, as the need for their services arose in some other town or part of the country; and they *could* switch jobs often, as their skill was much in demand, and their equipment was their talent only.

They had no investment in machinery, stock, or goodwill, and moved as the need for employment or change arose.

In a new locale the typesetters would seek out their own kind. After a day of work they would congregate in pubs or restaurants near work and socialize.

The only means they had for displaying their worth to each other were *social* means: conviviality, liberality, wit, good nature.

So they drank and talked, and the excellent man was one who could drink much, buy many rounds, and talk interestingly of the exploits of himself and others in the confraternity. The typesetter had no goods. He could not display excellence through the splendor of his carriage or his home.

He had no history except that which he invented for himself and could substantiate through bluff or humor.

He traveled light and carried few clothes, and so could not impress others by his wardrobe.

He could only establish his excellence through his social habits.

So he drank a lot.

Excellence in the theater is the art of giving things away.

The excellent actor strives not to *fix*, to codify, but to *create* for the moment, freely, without pausing either to corroborate what he or she has done or to appreciate the creation.

(This is why theatrical still photographs are many times stiff and uninteresting—the player in them is not *acting*, which is what he or she is trained and, perhaps, born to do, but *posing—indicating feelings*—which is the opposite of acting.)

A life in the theater is a life spent giving things away.

It is a life mobile, unstable, unsure of employment, of acceptance.

The future of the actor is made uncertain not only by chance, but by necessity—*intentionally*.

Our problems—like the problems of any professional group—are unique.

Our theatrical drolleries, necessities, and peculiarities may be diverting to others, but they are fascinating to ourselves.

The question of who did what to *whom*, who forgot his lines, what the producer said to the propman, who got and lost what part to whom and *why* ("This is the *real* story. I was *there*") is the endlessly interesting inquiry.

We in the theater tell stories about and on ourselves and our colleagues, and these stories are exactly the same ones Aristophanes told to and on his friends. They are attributed to different personalities, but the stories are the same. The problems and the rewards are the same.

It is important to tell and retell stories, as the only real history of the ephemeral art is an oral history; everything fades very quickly, and the only surety is the word of someone who was there—who *talked* to someone who was there, who vouches for the fact that someone told him she had spoken to a woman who knew someone who was there.

It all goes very quickly, too.

Apprenticeship becomes rewarded with acceptance or rejection. This seems to happen overnight, and the event we have decided on as the turning point in a career was, looking back, quite probably not it at all.

A life in the theater is a life with the attention directed outward, and memory and the substantiation of others is very important.

We acquire skills through constant practice. They accrue in increments so small that we seem to be making no progress. We lose competence in the same way—taking for granted our hard-won habits and barely aware they are leaving us.

At the end of a performance, or the end of a season, the only creation the performer has left is him- or herself. This, and artifacts: clippings, programs.

Which is, perhaps, one reason we love stories.

"Do you remember . . . ?" also must mean, "*I* remember. *Don't* I?"

At the Neighborhood Playhouse School of the Theatre, Sanford Meisner said, "When you go into the professional world, at a stock theater somewhere, backstage, you will meet an older actor—someone who has been around awhile.

"He will tell you tales and anecdotes about life in the theater.

"He will speak to you about your performance and the performances of others, and he will generalize to you, based on his experience and his intuitions, about the laws of the stage. Ignore this man."

Not only do these people exist, but as one continues a theatrical career, one has a tendency to turn into them. At least I find that I do.

We certainly all need love. We all need diversion, and we need friendship in a world whose limits of commitment (a most fierce commitment) is most times the run of the play.

Camus says that the actor is a prime example of the Sisyphean nature of life.

This is certainly true, and certainly not novel, and *additionally* there is this: a life in the theater need not be an analogue to "life." It *is* life.

It is the choice and calling of a substantial number of persons—craftspersons and artists—and has been for a very long time.

My play, *A Life in the Theater,* is, though I may have led you to believe otherwise, a comedy about this life.

It is an attempt to look with love at an institution we all love, The Theater, and at the only component of that institution (about whom our feelings are less simple), the men and women of the theater—the world's heartiest mayflies, whom we elect and appoint to live out our dreams upon the stage.

CONCERNING
THE WATER ENGINE

We Americans know the real news never reaches the newspapers. We know the interests it affects are much too powerful to allow events which might disrupt the status quo to be truthfully reported in the press.

We each have our own notion as to who, in fact, killed Kennedy, and who killed Lincoln; as to what actually happened to the Lindbergh baby, or at the Bay of Pigs; as to how much Nixon actually knew.

But we do not look to the press for ratification of our beliefs. We believe gossip before we believe journalism, and we are much more likely to accept as true the statement of the relative of the cabdriver who heard Politician X say so-and-so in his cab than to accept the politician's broadcast statements meant for our consumption.

We believe the word of a human being whom we can look in the eye—however much his testimony rests on hearsay— before the statements of a faceless press.

Myths and fables live on without advertising—without the backing of high-powered interests—with no one profiting from their retelling.

The only profit in the sharing of a myth is to those who participate as storytellers or as listeners, and this profit is the shared experience itself, the *celebration* of the tale, and of its truth.

We believe that Edith Wilson ran the country in her husband's name while he was comatose, and that she forged his signature to documents of state; that we've had contact with intelligence from foreign worlds, and that our government's suppressed the information; that, somewhere, someone's found a cure for cancer; that Roosevelt let Lindbergh into Hauptmann's cell before the execution; that some governmental agency killed Martin Luther King.

These beliefs are part of our oral history. They are neither more nor less true than those things which we read in the press.

They are, however, more steadfastly believed.

Our distrust of institutions is great and well founded.

We're always ready to believe the worst of them because we know we'll never *know* the worst.

One of our hardiest and most beloved myths is that of *suppression* by the government, or by an industrial pseudo-government, of discoveries or of inventions which could improve our lives.

We have all heard stories, told both as fact and as fiction, of the light bulb which would not burn out, of runless stockings, of the pill which made gasoline when dropped in water, of the cheap patent drug which would cure the cold...

These myths of suppression ring true to us because we distrust institutions.

We feel malevolence in their lack of accountability.

We cannot *talk* to them. Who *is* "The Government"?

Who is "Big Business"?

We feel these faceless monoliths can only wish us harm.

We cannot look them in the eye. They're not accountable, and in this lack of accountability we feel danger, we feel they're capable of anything, and we express this feeling in our myths.

Tolstoy wrote that the only time human beings treat each

other without pity is when they have banded into institutions.

Buttressed by an institution, he said, we will perpetrate gross acts of cruelty and savagery and call it "performance of our duty," and feel absolutely no necessity of judging our own actions.

The code of an institution ratifies us in acting amorally, as any guilt which might arise out of our acts would be borne not by ourself, but shared out through the institution.

We have it somehow in our nature, Tolstoy wrote, to perform horrendous acts which we would never dream of as individuals, and think if they are done in the name of some larger group, a *state*, a *company*, a *team*, that these vile acts are somehow magically transformed, and become praiseworthy.

The Water Engine is an American fable about the common person and the institution.

It is set in Chicago during the Depression—in the second year of the Century of Progress Exposition, a celebration of technology.

The story starts like this: "In September 1934, a young man in Chicago, Illinois, designed and built an engine which used distilled water as its only fuel."

DECAY:
SOME THOUGHTS FOR ACTORS

THEODORE SPENCER MEMORIAL LECTURE,
HARVARD, FEBRUARY 10, 1986

We live in a very confusing time.

Many simple words seem to have lost their meaning, and many simple processes are being called by new words.

In neologisms and circumlocutions we seek to deny the essentially finite nature of the terrifying processes to which these words refer.

We speak of *relationships* rather than *marriage*.

We speak of *parenting* instead of *raising a child*; of *defense* as if the goal of defense were not the *elimination* or *negation* of a threat, which threat, of course, being eliminated would do away with the necessity of defense.

We speak of *progress* and *growth* as we speak of parenting. As processes without an object. We are afraid to think of the results of what we do. We refer to growth in the economy, growth in the "self," growth in relationships, as if one could progress except toward a specific goal, or grow except to mature. Hence these terms, progress and growth, used in a sense of infinite expansion, deny the idea of *completion* and *rest*.

But what *grows* must, at some point, *cease* growing. And, following a period of maturity, must decay and die.

Decay is an inevitable part of life, and the attempt to deny the existence of death is evidence of either an immature or a disturbed understanding.

Things grow over time. We do not conceive and deliver in the same instant; we cannot take in and give out at the same time. There is a time to accumulate and there is a time to disperse, and the final disassembly is decay, which takes place so that new life may take place.

The study of natural growth and decay is the study of The Theater; and theatrical organisms: a career, a play, a season, an institution, grow and mature and decay and die according to the same rules which govern the growth and death of a plant or an animal. The organism grows toward a set point, and is shaped by the resistance it encounters on the way to its predetermined goal.

The ambitions which bring a group of young people together in an urge to buck the odds and start a new company will eventually shake that company apart, as the ambitions, *when one set of goals has been reached*, carry the individuals involved to new conquests and so on.

All plays are about decay. They are about the ends of a situation which has achieved itself fully, and the inevitable disorder which ensues until equilibrium is again established.

This is why the theater has always been essential to human psychic equilibrium. The theater exposes us to the notion of decay, to the necessity of change: in comedy to the tenuousness of our social state, in tragedy to the inevitability of death. It is a constant human need, to dramatize, and the question, Is the theater dead? is not a request for information, but the expression of a deep personal anxiety (as, "Momma, are we going to have to move to a smaller apartment?"). "Is the theater dead?" means, Am *I* dead?

The dramatists and the play strive to create order out of a disordered state. Their job is to observe and enact decay as it leads to its conclusion of *rest*, and offer the solace, the conclusion appropriate to that rest. (In fables or cautionary tales: "So be careful what you do"; in melodrama, "So be assured that your emotions are intact, and these bind you to the rest of the people in the theater.")

During a period of growth, disorder is caused by *lack of completion*; the organism, the play, the tree grows till it is complete. Having completed itself, the process is reversed and order can only be restored by disassembly of the organism.

When a society is *growing* (just as when a play is growing) all aspects of that society promote growth: the arts, the economy, religion (as in nineteenth-century America). When a society is *growing* those things appear and thrive which will make the organism strong, virile, happy, outward-directed—*seminal*, in short. And we have all had this experience when working on a new project: we do without sleep, people who will help us miraculously appear, we master new skills easily, people are glad to meet us. . . .

When the society has achieved itself, all aspects of that society tend toward *disassembly*, toward reducing that society into its smallest component parts, so that rest can be achieved and those components can be employed in a new task.

When a society has achieved itself, has achieved its inscrutable purposes, it is not "bad luck" but common sense that all aspects of the society promote war, waste, pollution, doubt, anxiety—those things will hasten decay. (The operation of this decay can be seen simply by looking at a small society, a theater company, or a business. It becomes successful, the members get ambitious, bickering ensues, previously close relationships degenerate, no one shares the same opinion, monied interests appear to offer the going concern large amounts to stop what it is doing [franchising, etc.].)

When we look at our large society today we see many problems—overcrowding, the risk of nuclear annihilation, the perversion of the work ethic, the disappearance of tradition, homosexuality, sexually transmitted diseases, divorce, the tenuousness of the economy—and we say, "What bad luck that they are besetting us at once."

Even taken individually these occurrences seem incomprehensible. Taken as a whole the contemplation of them can surely induce terror. What is happening here and why have all these things, coincidentally, beset us?

Like many things which seem insoluble as problems, these things can be viewed also as solutions. They are an attempt to find rest.

Consider friendship which has run its course. Out of nowhere, an incident flares up, something nonsensical, over which friends take sides, and which ultimately tears the friendship apart. The problems which beset us are an attempt of the universe to, by natural selection, if you will, discover that one thing which will bring about a state of rest.

The problems of the world, AIDS, cancer, nuclear war, pollution, are, finally, no more solvable than the problems of a tree which has borne fruit: the apples are overripe and they are falling—what can be done? The leaves, coincidentally, are falling, too, just at the time when they are needed most; and the tree, already weakened, is being weighted down with ice, and the very sap which might sustain the valiant fight to keep life in the tree is draining. What can be done? What can be done about the problems which beset our life? *Nothing* can be done, and nothing needs to be done. Something *is* being done—the organism is preparing to rest.

We, as a culture, as a civilization, are at the point where the appropriate, the life-giving, task of the organism is to decay. Nothing will stop it, nothing *can* stop it, for it is the force of life, and the evidence is all around us. Listen to the music in train stations and on the telephone when someone puts you on hold. The problem is not someone or some group of people unilaterally deciding to plague you with bad music; the problem is a growing universal and concerted attempt to limit the time each of us is alone with his or her thoughts; it is the collective unconscious suggesting an act of mercy.

Now, how long will this tendency toward final rest take, this dissolution of the civilization? One day, one hour, perhaps, a year, a hundred years, certainly not more. And our civilization could dissolve, as people my age have known all their lives; it could happen at any time, and in one moment.

Where is the peace in this knowledge? Perhaps in this: as the Stoics said, either gods exist or they do not exist. If they exist, then, no doubt, things are unfolding as they should; if they do *not* exist, then why should we be reluctant to depart a world in which there are no gods?

And what about in the short view: most of you young people have more diverting and more appropriate things to do than burden yourselves with too much philosophy.

In the short view, life goes on, and there *is* a reason you are here; there is a reason our civilization grew, and there is a reason it is going to die—and those reasons are as unavailable to us as the reasons *we* were born and are going to die.

We need not fall victim to the liberal fallacy of assuming that because we can perceive a problem we are, de facto, not part of the problem. We are the problem, like the man driving home from the Hamptons on Sunday night and cursing the idiots who have caused the traffic jam. We are part of the process, the world is decaying rather rapidly, and there is *nothing* we can do about it.

Let's face it and look at it: how is our parochial world decaying? The theater has few new plays and most of them are bad. The critics seem to thwart originality and the expression of love at every turn; television buys off the talented; the art of acting degenerates astoundingly each year.

You younger people in the theater might say: Where is the kind and generous producer? The insightful talent agent? The wise critic? Better stop looking for them and assume they don't exist. Today the job of the agent, the critic, the producer, is *to hasten decay*, and they are doing their job—the job the society has elected them to do is *to spread terror* and the eventual apathy which ensues when an individual is too afraid to look at the world around him. They are the music in the railroad station, and they represent our desire for rest.

You might say what of free will in all this, what about the will of the individual? But I don't believe it exists, and I believe all societies function according to the rules of natural selection and that those survive who serve the society's turn, much like people stranded when their bus has broken down. Their individual personalities are unimportant; the necessity of the moment *will* create the expert, the reasonable man, the brash bully, the clown, and so on.

Now, what about *your* job?

Most of you who decide to stay in the theater will become part of the maelstrom of commercials, television, the quest for fame and recognition. In this time of decay those things which society will reward with fame and recognition are bad acting, bad writing, choices which inhibit thought, reflection, and release; and these things will be called art.

Some of you are born, perhaps, to represent the opposing view—the minority opinion of someone who, for whatever reason, is not afraid to examine his state. Some of you, in spite of it all, are thrown up by destiny to attempt to bring *order* to the stage, to attempt to bring to the stage, as Stanislavsky put it, the life of the human soul.

Like Laocoön, you will garner quite a bit of suffering in your attempts to perform a task which you will be told does not even exist. Please try to keep in mind that the people who tell you that, who tell you you are dull and talentless and noncommercial, are doing *their* job; and also bear in mind that, in your obstinacy and dedication, you are doing *your* job.

If you strive to bring order to the stage, if you strive to re-create in yourself that lost art of acting, the lost art of stagecraft, that ten-thousand-year-old art which has disappeared, for the large part, within my lifetime, if you strive to teach yourself the lost art of storytelling, you are going to suffer, and, as you work and age, you may look around you and say, "Why bother?" And the answer is you must bother if you are selected to bother, and if not, *then* not.

It is a very confusing world. So, as the Stoics say, we might all try to keep our principles few and simple, so that we may refer to them quickly. If you can keep in touch with natural processes, with yourself and your God, with the natural rudiments of your profession—the human necessity to tell and hear stories—with the natural process of growth and decay, then you can, I think, find peace, even in the theater.

Our civilization is convulsed and dying, and it has not yet gotten the message. It is sinking, but it has not sunk into complete barbarity, and I often think that nuclear war exists for no other reason than to spare us that indignity.

We might have wished these things not to be the case, but they *are* the case; and, for you young people, to quote Marcus Aurelius again: you receive a bad augury before a battle, *so what*? It's *still* your job to fight.

Those of you who are called to strive to bring a new theater, the theater of your generation, to the stage, are set down for a very exciting life.

You will be pulling against an increasingly strong current, and as you do so, you will reap the great and priceless reward of knowing yourself a truly mature man or woman—if, in the midst of the panic which surrounds you, and calls itself common sense, or commercial viability, you are doing your job simply and well.

If you are going to work in the true theater, that job is a great job in this time of final decay; that job is to bring to your fellows, through the medium of your understanding and skill, the possibility of communion with what is essential in us all: that we are born to die, that we strive and fail, that we live in ignorance of why we were placed here, and, that, in the midst of this we need to love and be loved, but we are afraid.

If you are blessed with intelligence you will find yourself in a constant battle between will and fear. Please know that this battle is exposure to the central aspect of drama: the battle between what you are called to do and what you would *rather* do. Exposure to this battle is an education in tragedy.

Your attempts to answer the question, "What must I do?" may lead you to embrace and study both philosophy and technique; to learn to meditate and to learn to act, so that your personality and your work become one, and you fulfill your true purpose, your highest purpose, as a member of the theater. And that purpose is this and has *always* been this: to represent culture's need to address the question, How can I live in a world in which I am doomed to die?

NOTES ON
THE CHERRY ORCHARD

When playing poker it is a good idea to determine what cards your opponents might hold. There are two ways to do this. One involves watching their idiosyncrasies—the way they hold their cards when bluffing as opposed to the way they hold them when they have a strong hand; their unconscious self-revelatory gestures; the way they play with their chips when unsure. This method of gathering information is called looking for "tells."

The other way to gather information is to analyze your opponent's hand according to what he *bets*.

These two methods are analogous—in the Theater—to a concern with *characterization*, and a concern with *action*; or, to put it a bit differently: a concern with the *way* a character does something and, on the other hand, the actual *thing that he does*.

I recently worked on an adaptation of *The Cherry Orchard*.

My newfound intimacy with the play led me to look past the quiddities of the characters and examine what it is that they are actually doing. I saw this:

The title is a flag of convenience. Nobody in the play gives a damn about the cherry orchard.

In the first act Lyubov returns. We are informed that her

beloved estate is going to be sold unless someone acts quickly to avert this catastrophe.

She is told this by the rich Lopakhin. He then immediately tells her that he has a plan: cut down the cherry orchard, raze the house, and build tract housing for the summer people.

This solution would save (although alter) the estate.

Lopakhin keeps reiterating his offer throughout the play. Lyubov will not accept. Lopakhin finally buys the estate.

"Well," one might say, "one cannot save one's beloved cherry orchard by cutting it down." That, of course, is true. But in the text other alternatives are offered.

Reference is made to the rich aunt in Yaroslavl ("who is so very rich"), and who adores Lyubov's daughter, Anya. A flying mendicant mission is proposed but never materializes. The point is not that this mission is viewed as a good bet— it isn't—but that, if the action of the protagonist (supposedly Lyubov) were to save the cherry orchard, she would vehemently pursue and grasp *any* possibility of help.

The more real hope of salvation is fortuitous marriage. Gaev, Lyubov's brother, enumerates the alternatives: inheriting money, begging from the rich aunt, marrying Anya off to a rich man.

The first is idle wishing, and we've struck off the second, but what about the third alternative?

There's nobody much around for Anya. But what about her stepsister, Varya?

Varya, Lyubov's adopted daughter, is not only nubile, she is *in love*. With whom is she in love? She is in love with the very wealthy Lopakhin.

Why, hell. If I wanted to save *my* cherry orchard, and *my* adopted daughter was in love (and we are told that her affections are by no means abhorrent to their recipient) with the richest man in town, what would *I* do? What would *you* do? It's the easy way out, the play ends in a half hour, and everybody gets to go home early.

But Lyubov does not press this point either, though she

makes reference to it in every act. She does *not* press on to a happy marriage between Varya and Lopakhin. Nor, curiously, is this match ever mentioned as a solution for the problem of the cherry orchard. The problem of the botched courtship of Varya and Lopakhin exists only as one of a number of supposed subplots. (More of this later.)

In the penultimate scene of the play, Lyubov, who is leaving her now-sold estate to return to Paris, attempts to tie up loose ends. She exhorts Lopakhin to propose to Varya, and he says he will. Left alone, Lopakhin loses his nerve and does not propose. Why does Lyubov, on learning this, not press her case? Why did she not do so sooner?

Even now, at the end of the play, if Lyubov *really* cared about the cherry orchard, she could save it from the ax. She could easily *force* Lopakhin to propose to Varya, and then get the bright idea that all of them could live on the estate as one happy family. And Lopakhin, who reveres her, would not refuse her.

But she does not do so. Is this from lack of inventiveness? No. It is from lack of concern. The cherry orchard is not her concern.

What about Lopakhin? Why is *he* cutting down the cherry orchard? He has been, from his youth, infatuated with Lyubov. She is a goddess to him, her estate is a fairyland to him, and his great desire in the play is to please her. (In fact, if one were to lapse into a psychological overview of the play at this point, one might say that the reason Lopakhin can't propose to Varya is that he is in love with Lyubov.)

Lopakhin buys the estate. For ninety thousand rubles, which means nothing to him. He then proceeds to cut down the trees, which he knows will upset his goddess, Lyubov, and to raze the manor house. His parents were slaves in that house; Lyubov grew up in the house; he doesn't need the money; why is he cutting down the trees? (Yes, yes, yes, we encounter halfhearted addenda in regard to future generations being won back to the land. But it doesn't wash. Why? If

Lopakhin wanted to build a summer colony, he could build it anywhere. He could have built it without Lyubov's land and without her permission. If his objective were the building of summer homes and he were faced with two tracts, one where he had to cut down his idol's home, and one where he did not, which would he pick? Well, he has an infinite number of tracts. He can build anywhere he wants. Why cut down the trees and sadden his beloved idol? Having bought the estate he could easily let it sit, and, should the spirit move him subsequently, build his resort elsewhere.)

What, in effect, is going on here?

Nothing that has to do with trees.

The play is a series of scenes about sexuality, and, particularly, frustrated sexuality.

The play was inspired, most probably, by the scene in *Anna Karenina* between Kitty's friend Mlle Varenka and her gentleman companion Koznyeshev. The two of them, lonely, nice people, are brought together through the office of mutual friends. Each should marry, they are a perfect match. In one of the finest scenes in the book we are told that each knew the time had arrived, that it was Now or Never. They go for a walk, and Mr. Koznyeshev is about to propose when he is distracted by a question about mushrooms. And so the two nice people are doomed to loneliness.

If this description sounds familiar, it should. Chekhov, pregnant of his theme, lifted it shamelessly (and probably unconsciously) from Tolstoy and gave it to Lopakhin and Varya.

Not only do Lopakhin and Varya play out the scene, *everybody in the play plays out the same scene.*

Anya is in love with Pyotr Trofimov, the tutor of her late brother. Trofimov is in love with *her*, but is too repressed to make the first move. He, in fact, declares that he is above love, while, in a soliloquy, refers to Anya as "My springtime, my dear Morning Sun."

Yepihodov, the estate bookkeeper, is in love with Dunyasha, the chambermaid. He keeps trying to propose, but she thinks him a boor and will not hear him out. *She* is in love with Yasha, Lyubov's footman. Yasha seduces and abandons her, as he is in love with himself.

Lyubov herself is in love. She gave her fortune to her paramour and nursed him through three years of his sickness. He deserted her for a younger woman.

Now, *this* is the reason she has returned to the estate. It is purely coincidental that she returns just prior to the auction of the orchard. *Why* is it coincidental? Because, as we have seen, she doesn't come back to *save* it. If she wanted to she could. *Why* does she come back? What is the event that prompts her return? Her jilting. What is the event that prompts her to return again to Paris? The continual telegrams of her roué lover begging for forgiveness.

Why did Lyubov come home? To lick her wounds, to play for time, to figure out a new course for her life.

None of these is a theatrically compelling action. (The last comes closest, but it could be done in seclusion and does not require other characters. As, indeed, the role of *Lyubov* is, essentially a monologue—there's nothing she *wants* from anyone on stage.)

If Lyubov is doing nothing but these solitary, reflective acts, why is she the protagonist of the play? She *isn't*.

The play has no protagonist. It has a couple of squad leaders. The reason it has no protagonist is that it has no through-action. It has one scene repeated by various couples.

To continue:

Lyubov's brother is Gaev. He is a perennial bachelor, and is referred to several times in the text as an Old Lady. What does *he* want? Not much of anything. Yes, he cries at the end when the orchard is cut down. But he appears to be just as happy going to work in the bank and playing caroms as he is lounging around the Morning Room and playing caroms.

The other odd characters are Firs, the ancient butler, who is happy the mistress has returned, and Simeonov-Pishchik, a poor neighbor who is always looking on the bright side.

Pishchik, Firs, and Gaev are local color. They are all celibate and seen as somewhat doddering in different degrees. And they are all happy. Because they are not troubled by Sex. They are not involved in the play's one and oft-repeated action: to consummate, clarify, or rectify an unhappy sexual situation.

The cherry orchard and its imminent destruction is nothing other than an effective dramatic device.

The play is not "If you don't pay the mortgage I'll take your cow." It is "Kiss me quick because I'm dying of cancer."

The *obstacle* in the play does not grow out of, and does not even *refer* to, the actions of the characters. The play works because it is a compilation of brilliant scenes.

I would guess—judging from its similarity to many of his short stories—that Chekhov wrote the scenes between the servant girl Dunyasha and Yepihodov first. That perhaps sparked the idea of a scene between Dunyasha and the man *she* loves, Yasha, a footman just returned from Paris. Who did this fine footman return with? The mistress. *Et ensuite.*

To continue this conceit: What did Chekhov do when he had two hours' worth of scenes and thirteen characters running around a country house? He had, as any playwright has, three choices. He could shelve the material as brilliant sketches; he could *examine* the material and attempt to discern any intrinsically dramatic through-action, and extrapolate the play out of *that*. Compare the structure of *The Cherry Orchard* with that of *The Seagull*. In *The Seagull*, the famous actress Arkadina wants to recapture her youth, which causes her to devote herself to a younger man and ignore the needs of her son, whose age is an affront to her pretensions of youth. He struggles to obtain her respect and the respect and love of Nina (another actress), who represents one split-off aspect of Arkadina's personality: her available sexuality. *The Seagull* is structured as a tragedy. At the end of the play the hero, Treplev, undergoes recognition of his state and reversal of his situation—he kills himself. What happens at the end of *The*

Cherry Orchard? Everyone goes home—they go back to doing *exactly* what they were doing before the play began. You might say *The Cherry Orchard* is structured as a *farce*. That is the dramatic form to which it is closest. One might also say that it is close to a series of review sketches with a common theme, and, in fact, it is. The play is most closely related to, and is probably the first example of, the twentieth-century phenomenon of the revue-play ... the *theme* play, for example, *La Ronde, Truckline Cafe, Men in White, Detective Story, Waters of the Moon*, etc.

To return: Chekhov has thirteen people stuck in a summer house. He has a lot of brilliant scenes. His third alternative is to come up with a pretext which will keep all thirteen characters in the same place and *talking* to each other for a while. This is one of the dilemmas of the modern dramatist: "Gosh, this material is *fantastic*. What can I do to just Keep the People in the House?"

One can have a piece of jewelry stolen. One can have a murder committed. One can have a snowstorm. One can have the car break down. One can have The Olde Estate due to be sold for debts in three weeks unless someone comes up with a good solution.

I picture this pretext occurring to Chekhov, and his saying, "Naaaa, they'll never go for it." I picture him watching rehearsals and *wincing* every time Lopakhin says (as he says frequently): "Just remember, you have only three (two, one) weeks until the cherry orchard is to be sold." Fine, he must have thought. That's real playwriting. One doesn't see Horatio coming out every five minutes and saying, "Don't forget, Hamlet, your uncle killed your dad and now he's sleeping with your ma!"

Oh, no, he must have thought, I'll never get away with it. But he did, and left us a play we cherish.

Why do we cherish the play? Because it is about the struggle between the Old Values of the Russian aristocracy and their loosening grasp on power? I think not. For, finally, a play is about—and is *only* about—the actions of its characters. We, as audience, understand a play not in terms of the superficial idiosyncrasies or social *states* of its characters (which, finally, *separate* us from the play), but only in terms of the *action* the characters are trying to accomplish. Set Hamlet in Waukegan and it's still a great play.

The enduring draw of *The Cherry Orchard* is not that it is set in a dying Czarist Russia or that it has rich folks and poor folks. We are drawn to the play because it speaks to our *subconscious*—which is what a play should do. And we subconsciously perceive and enjoy the reiterated action of this reiterated scene: two people at odds—each trying to fulfill his or her frustrated sexuality.

ACTING

We live in very selfish times. Nothing is given away free. Any impulse of creation or whimsy or iconoclasm which achieves general notice is immediately co-opted by risk capital, and its popularity—which arose from its generosity and freedom of thought—is made to serve the turn of financial extortion.

The successful workingman's café is franchised nationwide, and the charm of its artlessness wholesaled. The energy and invention of the bohemian quarter is transformed by promoters into the marketability of "Artland." The privacy of the remote seaside resort conducive to contemplation and renewal is sold piecemeal to millions of vacationers hungry for retreat who are willing to pay for a frantic, thronged pilgrimage to a spot where retreat was once possible.

It's not a very good time for the arts. And it is an especially *bad* time for the art of acting; for actors, as Hamlet told us, are "the abstract and brief chronicles of their time."

There are, of course, actors whose performances are hailed as great, because critics grade (as they must, in the absence of any aesthetic criteria) on the curve. But a comparison of that which contemporary journalism lauds as great acting with the great actors of the thirties and forties (Cary Grant, Garbo,

Henry Fonda, James Stewart, etc.) shows how drastically we have lowered our standards.

We expect less of our actors today because we expect less of ourselves.

Our attention is limited; and in this time of fear and anxiety, our attention is devoted to ourselves, our feelings, our emotions, our immediate well-being. This makes for *very* bad acting, as the more our attention is focused on ourselves the less interesting we become—think of how many fascinating hypochondriacs you know.

The laws of attention which are true off stage are true *on* stage. The self-concerned person is a bore and the self-concerned *actor* is a bore. And whether the actor is saying, "I must play this scene in order to be well thought of," *or*, "I must remember and re-create the time my puppy died in order to play this scene well," makes no difference. In both cases his attention is self-centered, and in both cases his performance will tell us nothing we couldn't have learned more enjoyably in a library.

Acting, as any art, must be generous; the attention of the artist must be focused outward—not on what he is feeling, but on what he is trying to accomplish.

The *organic* actor must have generosity and courage—two attributes which our current national hypochondria render in low supply and even lower esteem. He must have the courage to say to his fellow actors on stage (and so to the audience): "I am not concerned with influencing or *manipulating* you, I am not concerned with *nicety*. I am here on a mission and I *demand* you give me what I want."

This actor brings to the stage *desire* rather than completion, *will* rather than emotion. His performance will be compared not to *art*, but to *life;* and when we leave the theater after his performance we will speak of *our life* rather than *his technique*. And the difference between this organic actor and the self-concerned performer is the difference between a wood fire and a fluorescent light.

In a Golden Age, that which delights us on the stage (that acting we would call "art") would be the same things which delight us in our lives: simplicity, elegance, kindness, force— not that which is portrayed but that which allows us to infer; not the technical but the provocative. And in a Golden Age we would judge an actor's "character" on stage the exact same way we judge it off stage: not by his protestations and assurances but by his determination, his constancy of purpose, his generosity—in effect, his "goodness."

But we don't live in a Golden Age, and the actor, the Brief Chronicle, is an expression of and a servant to his times.

We have demanded of him and received of him little other than this: a continual portrayal and repetition of the idea that nothing very much is happening around us, that we need not worry, and that it is absolutely correct that our actions should *not* be determined by our perceptions.

We have demanded of the actor that he repeat to us constantly that it is fine to laugh when not amused, to cry when not moved, to beam gratitude upon the unacceptable, to condone the unforgivable, to express delight in the banal.

That most of today's acting is false and mechanical is no coincidence—it is a sign of our society's demanding that its priests repeat the catechism essential for our tenuous mental health: that nothing is happening, that nothing very bad or very good can befall us, that we are safe.

There are exceptions, of course. There are organic performances and organically directed productions and companies. But there aren't many. The actor works in a community, and the communal ideal of excellence is contagious and exigent.

Can we again ratify the Actor and the Theater which is organic rather than mechanical—which responds to our need to *love* rather than our need to *have*?

In this century the great and vital theaters (The Group in 1930s New York, Brecht's in 1920s Berlin, Stanislavsky's Art in 1900 Moscow, The Second City in 1960 Chicago) have emerged in response to, and signaling the end of, introverted, uncertain social periods.

For the moment, generous, organic acting can be seen occasionally in the theater (though seldom in the commercial theater), more regularly in film (generally in smaller roles), and most consistently as part of dance or opera, in performances given by those dedicated not to their *performances* but to the actions demanded by their material—in the work of Pavarotti or Baryshnikov, or Hildegarde Behrens, or Yuriko, or Fischer-Dieskau.

When, once again, actors are cherished and rewarded who bring to the stage or the screen generosity, desire, *organic life*, actions performed freely—without desire for reward or fear of either censure or misunderstanding—that will be one of the first signs that the tide of our introverted, unhappy time has turned and that we are once again eager and prepared to look at ourselves.

REALISM

Most American theatrical workers are in thrall to the idea of *realism*. A very real urge to be truthful, to be *true*, constrains them to judge their efforts and actions against an inchoate, which is to say against an *unspecified* standard of reality.

That the standard is unspecified is important, as it thus becomes the explanation and excuse for any action or effort the artist feels disinclined to make. It becomes a peremptory challenge.

A necessary response to the artist who says "It's not *true*" must be "True to what?"

Stanislavsky and, more notably, Vakhtangov suggested that—that to which the artist must be *true* is the aesthetic integrity of the play.

This places a huge responsibility on the artist. He or she faced with this charge—to care for the *scenic truth*—can no longer take refuge in a blanket dismissal or *endorsement* of anything on the grounds of its being not realistic.

In general, each facet of every production must be weighed and understood solely on the basis of its interrelationship to the other elements; on its service or lack of service to the meaning, the *action* of the play.

A chair is not *per se* truthful or untruthful. That one may say, "Yes, but it is a chair, an actual chair, people sit on it and I found it in a cafeteria, therefore it belongs in this play about a cafeteria," is beside the point. Why was that *particular* chair chosen? Just as that particular chair said something about the cafeteria *in* the cafeteria (its concern for looks over comfort, for economy over durability, etc.), so that chair, on stage, will say something *about the play*; so the question is: What do you, the theatrical director, wish to say *about the play*?

What does the chair mean *in the play*? Does it symbolize power? Then have *that* chair. Abasement? Possession, and so on. Choose the correspondingly appropriate chair. One might say, "Give it up, *it's just a chair....*" But, again, someone is going to *choose* it; shouldn't that someone *recognize* that he is consciously or unconsciously making a choice, and make the choice consciously, and in favor of an idea more specific to the play than the idea of "reality."

A conscious devotion to the *Idea* of a play is a concern for what Stanislavsky called the Scenic Truth, which is to say, the truth *in this particular scene*. The important difference between realism and truth, Scenic Truth, is the difference between acceptability and necessity, which is the difference between entertainment and Art.

So what if the play is set in a cafeteria? A cafeteria has no objective reality, as far as we artists are concerned. Our question is *why* is the play set in a cafeteria, what does it mean that the play is set in a cafeteria, and what *aspect* of this cafeteria is important *to the meaning of the play*. Having determined that, we may discard immediately all other aspects of the cafeteria and concentrate *only* on that which puts forward the meaning of the play. E.g.: if, in our particular play, the cafeteria means a place where the hero is always open to surveillance, the designer can build a set which reflects the idea: inability to hide. If the meaning of the cafeteria is a place where reflection and rest are possible, the designer's work can reflect *these* ideas. In neither case is the designer's first question: "What does a cafeteria look like?" His first question is: "What does it mean *in this instance?*" This is a concern for scenic truth.

In devotion to this Scenic Truth the artist gives him- or herself a choice. In discarding the armor of realism he or she accepts the responsibility of making every choice in light of specific *meaning*—of making every choice assertive rather than protective. For, in this age, to make a "realistic" choice, to assert that such and such a choice was made because it is, in fact, *as it is in life* is to say no more than that the choice was made in such a way as to avoid any potential criticism.

Everything which does not put forward the meaning of the play impedes the meaning of the play. To do too much or too little is to mitigate and weaken the meaning. The acting, the design, the direction should all consist only of that bare minimum necessary to put forward the action. Anything else is embellishment.

The problem of realism in design and its deleterious effects should be studied as a guide to the similar problem in acting. Actors for the last thirty years have been hiding in a ludicrously incorrect understanding of the Stanislavsky System and employing incorrectly understood jargon as an excuse for not acting.

Almost *never* are the teachings of Stanislavsky employed as an incitement; they are offered as an excuse—a substitute for action. The purpose of the system was, and is, to *free* the actor from extraneous considerations and permit him or her to turn all of his or her concentration to the objective, which is not "this performance," but the *meaning* of the play.

The notions of objective, activity, moment, beat, and so on are all devoted toward reducing the scene to a specific action which is true to the author's intention, and physically capable of being performed. The purpose of these concepts is to incite the actor to act. They all prod the actor to answer the one question which is capable of freeing him from self-consciousness and permitting him or her to become an artist: "What am I doing?"

The purpose of the Stanislavsky system of thought was to permit the actor to freely give the truth, the highest truth, of him- or herself, to the ideas, to the words of the playwright. The system teaches specificity as a tool of release rather than constraint. To make the transition from realism to truth, from self-consciousness to creativity, the artist must learn how to be specific to *something greater than him- or herself* on different levels of abstraction: the meaning of the scene, the intention of the author, the thrust of the play. But never "reality," or "truth," in general.

That to which one must learn to be true is not one's vision of reality, which, by its very nature, will make the actor more self-conscious and less able to act, but to the *aspirations* central to the meaning of the play and expressed in the objectives of the characters.

All theater is about aspirations—it is about longing and the desire for answers—small theater concerns itself with small questions, and great theater with great. In any case, the question at stake is never the *comfort* of the artist.

To have this never-ceasing concern with one's personal comfort, with the "naturalness" of the script, the blocking, the direction, the other actors, is to reduce every play to the *same* play—to a play about "That which I am not prepared to do" or "Those choices I will not make, and which I cannot be *forced* to make."

And so what?

Let us cast aside concerns of comfortability on stage. Why should one be comfortable acting Othello or St. Joan? The study of all theatrical artists should be action. *Movement.* A first test of all elements should be not "Do I feel comfortable (i.e., *immobile*) when considering it?" but "Do I feel *impelled*? Do I start to *move*? Does it make me want to *do* something?"

Actors are many times afraid of feeling foolish. We should teach each other to feel *power* rather than fear when faced with the necessity of choice, to seek out and enjoy, to feel the life-giving pleasure of the power of artistic choice.

AGAINST
AMPLIFICATION

Let's be serious for a moment.
If you are an actor and you can't make yourself heard in a
thousand-seat house, you're doing something wrong—you
should get off the stage and go home. Go back to voice class
or wherever your instincts lead you, but get off the stage.

Dramatic works are meant to be *acted*. They concern themselves with commitment and its consequences.

They cannot be delivered conversationally and then amplified—that is not *drama*, that is *television*.

Any actor, producer, writer, or director who thinks that
transistors and circuitry can fill the gap between the ability
of the artist and the needs of the audience is degrading all
concerned.

The correct, necessary, and only amplification needed in
e theater is the commitment of the artist (and here I mean
primarily the writer and the actor)—commitment sufficient,
if the case is that they cannot be heard, to send the one back
to the typewriter and the other back to the studio.

The writer who writes *behavior* rather than *drama*, of course,
has a need of actors who are miked, because that writer's
words are not going to awaken in the actor the *need to speak*—
the need to be heard.

The actor who permits him- or herself to be miked on the dramatic stage is destroying both art and livelihood—destroying the profession in much the same way that television has, which says to the artist, "It's sufficient for you just to get up there in front of the cameras and say the lines."

The art of the theater is action. It is the study of commitment. The word is an act. To *say* the word in such a way as to make it heard and understood by all in the theater is a commitment—it is the highest art to see a human being out on a stage speaking to a thousand of his or her peers saying, "These words which I am speaking are the *truth*—they are not an approximation of any kind. They are the God's truth, and I support them with my life," which is what the actor does on stage.

Without this commitment, acting becomes prostitution and writing becomes advertising.

The electronic amplification of the live stage is yet another wretched expediency which benefits no one but the speculator.

The beautiful, trained human voice and its extrapolation, live music, are the most beautiful and perfect sounds we will ever hear. Let us not participate in eliminating, through laziness, this beauty from our lives.

Let us assume responsibility for putting something on the stage worth saying—something the actors will feel moved to speak with commitment and something the audience will feel moved to listen to. That, traditionally, has been the limit of our responsibility.

But I think that today we have a responsibility to oppose this sonic garbage in the theater, to oppose it every way we can.

We can specify in individual contracts that our plays are not to be amplified; we can bring a resolution to the council to decry and/or investigate positive means to reverse this trend; we can be vocal about it in public and in print—the audience could use some educating on this score; they are being robbed and they don't know it.

I know some of you are thinking that I'm vastly overstating the case. I feel this issue, *far* beyond threatening the purity of the theater, threatens its very integrity.

Neil Simon said that the laugh track killed television comedy because the writers no longer needed to be funny.

Electronic amplification is killing and will kill the Broadway stage because the actors and the writers will no longer need to speak out.

ADDRESS TO THE
AMERICAN THEATER CRITICS
CONVENTION

AT THE TYRONE GUTHRIE THEATER,
MINNEAPOLIS, MINNESOTA, AUGUST 25, 1978

*If only the stage were as high and narrow as a tightrope, so that
only those completely trained would dare to venture out on it.*
— Sanford Meisner

The first task of the actor, the
first lesson, and one of the hardest, is to learn to take criticism—to learn to view self-consciousness as a tool for *bet-
tering* the self, rather than as a tool for *protecting* the self.
Mastery of this lesson is essential if one is to learn to look
dispassionately at what he or she has done.

One must look honestly at what one has done, and to
compare it to what one was *trying* to do. To learn useful
mechanical lessons from the comparison is difficult; many
workers in the theater never learn to do it.

Not to know how to make this comparison is the mark of
an amateur. It is the mark of a person to whom the theater
is, finally, a diversion rather than a profession, and it is the
mark of a person who wants the theater to give to *him* or *her*,
but wants to give nothing in return.

One of the worst things that can befall a beginning, an
untrained actor is to be ratified, to be praised for idiosyncrasies—for those things which, given time and technique,

might become strengths, but in the absence of these are no more than eccentricities.

If one has no ability or inclination to scrutinize what he or she does *in terms of greater goals*, to be ratified early can be, and usually is, stultifying.

It is especially stultifying when accompanied, as often happens, by blandishments to the effect that there is no such thing as technique; that there *is* no need to study; that the only way to learn is through doing; and that, finally, pursuit of good habits of work, that is, technique, and good habits of thought, that is, philosophy, are effete.

This advice to "do what one does so well" causes a well-known inversion. It creates in the performer a necessary interest in "know-nothingism," and he or she comes to deny the very existence of both technique and of aesthetic. He or she becomes, in effect, a fascist, a complete egocentric who is the champion of "doing what I feel," "saying what I feel," "writing what I feel."

And the result is more or less harmful garbage.

The garbage is, of course, all the more harmful when it is the product of some incipient "talent" on the part of the creator, as the talent will make the product a little bit more attractive, though no less unworthy. But there *is* such a thing as technique. And a career in the theater must have long-range technical and philosophic goals. And these cannot be egocentric goals.

Without these goals one does not have the strength or the distance for moment-to-moment honest self-criticism, and without this self-critique there is no improvement and there is no happiness.

Performers who lack the ability to criticize themselves, who take no responsibility for understanding *what it is that they do* and the moral and mechanical precepts to which they must adhere, are not happy. Not one.

They are confused by success and humiliated by failure, and they are always looking for someone either to kiss their ass or to hold their hand, and well they might, for they, naturally, have no faith in themselves and they are not happy. They make themselves unhappy by denying themselves the comfort of anything *greater* than themselves. They are sterile.

So with the performer in the theater, and so with you, the theatrical critics. If you do not learn your craft, the Theater, and its moral and practical precepts, if you do not make this your constant study, if you do not learn to judge yourselves against a standard of artistic perfection and amend your works day to day in light of that standard, you *must* be unhappy.

Just as with the performer. If you trust outside plaudits and support for your work, you are being controlled. Your life is not your own. Just as is evidenced in that sick moment when you have a deadline to make and not a thing in the world to say, and you think not *what must I say about that piece*, but *what would be acceptable*, or *witty*, or *nouveau*.

Many of you, as with performers, treat the theater as your personal beat—your personal amusement and nothing greater than a shooting mark which will enable you to display your expertise.

My question to you is this: Would you not be happier as a *part* of the theater?

If your answer (and it may be hidden in your secret heart) is yes, then treat the theater with love. We, as members of the community, have the right to demand this of an actor, or director, or writer, or designer, and we have the right to demand it of a critic, for, barring this, the critic in question is not *of the theater*, but is an exploiter, no matter what title he or she goes by.

Treat the theater with love and devotion sufficient to learn some of its rudimentary fiats.

Learn your craft and be part of the theater, for, while you are learning and striving to write better and to write more informedly and to write more in light of a standard of artistic perfection, you are as much a part of the theater as anyone else in it—now or in antiquity; and while you are *not* striving to improve and to write informedly and morally and to a purpose, you are a hack and a plaything of your advertisers.

Study acting; it is a fascinating study. If you are uneducated in its techniques, you are incapable of distinguishing good from bad—unless you are prepared to fall back on that old saw, "I know what I like," or, "I write for the popular taste of my subscribers," which is to say, "for a hypothetical person dumber than I am"; and if that is what you are doing, you are in serious trouble and insulting yourself and the people who read your publication.

And I say to you: write for *yourself*, and be an artist.

Study theater history. Teach yourself some perspective, so that you are not at the mercy of the current *fad*, which is another levy of "I know what I like."

Study voice and movement—learn the difference between the beautiful and the attractive.

Learn to analyze a script the way a director should and almost none can.

Make *yourself* the expert, and let us lay to rest the critic as *weather vane* and reporter to the *public taste*, which is only a fiction in the minds of knaves.

Study the theater. Your friends will tell you you are making yourself foolish—that you are wasting your time and no one will appreciate the finer points in any case. And this is exactly what bad actors say to devoted actors.

Love the theater and learn about it and strive to improve it and create a *new* profession for yourselves. The profession of the "theater critic" is debauched, but you don't have to be debauched.

Train yourself for a profession that *does not exist*. That is the mark of an *artist*—to create something which formerly existed only in his or her heart.

OBSERVATIONS OF
A BACKSTAGE WIFE

Iceman *is a science-fiction film which was released in the summer of 1984. It is about a group of research scientists in the Arctic who discover and revive a 20,000-year-old Neanderthal man they have found frozen in a glacier. It was filmed during the four months of February– May 1983 on locations in Churchill, Manitoba, and Stewart, British Columbia, and in studios in Vancouver, British Columbia. The film stars Tim Hutton and Lindsay Crouse. As Ms. Crouse's husband, I spent much of the shoot in Canada with the film, and was privileged to enjoy the companionship of the cast and crew and the courtesy of the production company.*

On location we are isolated. We are like people whose bus has broken down—we are going to have to choose temporary roles and make the best of it for a while.

A traditional hierarchy of power controls most relationships in the entertainment industry, but that hierarchy holds its most powerful sway back at home. At home we are divided by craft-within-the-industry (the directors don't live next door to the technicians), by income, and by achievement. Here, on location, everyone's lumped together twenty-four hours a day for four months.

The recognition symbols which give us power at home don't do the trick up here ("Okay, that's *still* a Patek Philippe watch; I saw it yesterday. What else can you do?"). Most of the perquisites of money have been eliminated in towns in which there is nothing to buy.

Life on location is a Clean Slate. We have entered Tombstone Territory and, to a large extent, are free to invent identities for ourselves and for the group as a whole.

The cast and crew had just arrived on Hudson Bay, in Churchill, Manitoba. It was February, and constantly 40 to 50 degrees below zero.

My wife was staying at the Tundra Inn, and I called to see how she was doing. The friendly hotel operator said, "They're all in the bar," and put the phone down while she paged my wife. I heard much raucous laughter in the background; then my wife came to the phone. "Well," I said, "what's it like up there?" There was a pause and then she said, "It's like Film Camp."

PROFESSIONAL HIERARCHY

Joe Somer and Richard Monette are two of the featured actors in the movie. We are taking a several-hours' walk down a seemingly endless sandpit in the Portland Canal outside Stewart, British Columbia. We are taking this walk as there is absolutely nothing to do in this town.

Outside of the Alpine Motel, where half of the cast and crew is lodged, is a vacant lot full of mud. On the weekends, many inhabitants of Stewart drive their four-wheel-drive vehicles through and around the mud lot, hoping to get stuck and then become unstuck. If we had such vehicles we would, no doubt, join them. Having none, we complain about the noise they make and find our excitement where we can. This afternoon our excitement is a walk.

Monette avers that this is the only town in the world whose cultural life would be improved by a nuclear war. "I rather like it," says Somer. "Do come by for tea this afternoon, will you, I'm at the Edward..." "In the Terrace or the Lounge?" asks Monette.

The "Edward" is the King Edward Hotel, a rather basic cinder-block affair on the town's one short street.

And so we pass the time playing the dozens on the "Edward" and Far Northern Life in general. Monette had created something of a cultural stir the day before by producing a copy of *Huck Finn* he found on a rack in the back of the town's shoe store. He announced the store had several copies left. All of them disappeared by that evening.

There is *nothing* to do in this town in which we are very much strangers, and bitching—if only for the moment—turns homesickness and boredom into a sense of exclusivity.

When the thrill of dishing the "Edward" wanes, Monette takes up the leitmotif of the helicopter. He is slated, when weather permits, to do a shot hanging out of the door of a helicopter airborne over the glacier.

In the shot a stuntman, dressed as the Neanderthal, hangs on the skid of the airborne helicopter. A second stuntman jumps from the plane and free-falls with a camera. He films the Neanderthal stuntman, who then loses his grip on the skid and falls while Monette leans out of the door and tries to save him.

Monette does not like flying, doesn't like the idea of helicopters, and doesn't like the fact that he has agreed to do the shot.

Joe Somer and I concur with all his reservations. It seems to us all that Monette's part of the shot should be played by a stuntman who has been both trained and rewarded for undertaking this kind of danger. Monette is neither, and is hiding his anxiety beneath a display of anxiety.

Somer suggests Monette go to the town pharmacist and explain that everyone back in his hometown has a toothache and could he please have eight million Percodans. As he is speaking, one of the film trucks pulls up and Warren Carr, the second assistant director, leans out and tells Monette to saddle up, as the weather has cleared and he is going for a helicopter ride.

We all drive back to the airstrip, where we watch Monette rehearse the shot (on the ground) with the stunt crew. At the airstrip, Norman Jewison, who with Patrick Palmer is producing the film, is consulting with the pilots. This is a very important, very expensive shot, and the producers are on hand to see that it goes well or to have been there if it goes badly.

Jewison nods to Monette who says, joking in earnest, that he hopes Jewison will remember this favor when casting his next film. Jewison, distracted by the logistics of the shot, smiles and moves on.

Jewison will almost certainly *not* remember Monette when casting his next film. This is no particular reflection on Norman Jewison—it is just the way things are in the Biz: a thing's worth is identical with its price, and Monette is doing the stunt as a favor.

So, amazingly, in spite of the recent Vic Morrow tragedy (the deaths of several actors, two of them children, in a helicopter accident while filming) and the great clamor it created in the trade press for strict adherence to industry safety codes; in spite of the fact that he *knows* that a producer will usually consider the granting of a favor a display of contemptible weakness, Monette will do the shot.

In Vaudeville Times, legitimate actors were known as the Harold and Arthurs. Monette, Crouse, Joe Somer, and I were very much Harold and Arthurs on location. We are from the East, and each came to the movies first having spent one or two decades working in the theater.

We are *specifically* conditioned to consider ourselves subservient to directors and producers: the director passes out the work and the producer hands out the paycheck. Most actors make a virtue of necessity and, being members of a profession which prizes gentility and courtesy, treat directors and producers with such. And it is good to know one's place.

Monette is a fine actor; he doesn't want to gum up the works. He is also a considerate man and has been asked a favor. Though scared stiff, he did the stunt.

Joe Somer and I left the airstrip and strolled over to the old, abandoned Empress Hotel, which is being used as our soundstage. At the Empress, we watch Fred Schepisi, the film's director, shooting a scene with Lindsay Crouse. He finishes the scene and shouts, generally, "Where's Richard Monette?" Nobody on the set knows. "He's up in a helicopter," Somers says.

"Up in the helicopter," says Schepisi. "Isn't that *danger-ous . . . ?*"

FUN ON LOCATION

That evening Monette, safely returned, is celebrating his new-won wings with a lobster dinner at the Edward. He regales us with the story of his life in the clouds.

There were four men in the helicopter: Monette and the pilot in the cockpit proper, and Dar Robinson and Carl Lob-urn, the two stuntmen, in a separate compartment at the rear of the aircraft.

At the assigned altitude the two stuntmen walked out along the skid to the front of the plane. The cameraman jumped, free-falling and filming while the second stuntman (dressed as the Neanderthal), hung on to the skid. Monette, secured by two seat belts, leaned out of the open door attempting to "save" the Neanderthal, who lost his grip and fell from the skid.

The stunt successfully completed, Monette closed the door and leaned happily back in his seat while the pilot flew him back to the airstrip. Several moments later, his happy reverie was broken by the sound of someone frantically banging on the outside of the helicopter window. Monette turned to see the face of a completely unknown individual leering at him from outside the helicopter. This person then waved bye bye, jumped from the skid, and free-fell to within a very scant number of feet from the ground, where he opened a parachute. This was a third member of the stunt team—a parachute packer—who came along unannounced and thought he would enliven everybody's day.

At night most of the company walked or bused the two miles across the American border into Hyder, Alaska, which looks like a derivative and not very effective student scenic design project: "The Western Town, 1850." Main Street has three bars, the border customs station (which was never manned), and a gift shop.

GROUP IDENTITY

As a company, we were quite taken with souvenirs. They validate our travels and they fix us as a group. They are our uniforms. In Churchill, Manitoba, the company's location before Stewart ("Churchill: the Polar Bear Capital of the world. Our household pests are ten feet tall and weigh half a ton"), the local industry was fur and the company got off the plane from Churchill in wolf parkas, vests, hats, moose mukluks, and (John Lone, the Iceman himself) in a massive black bear parka. Lone quite literally stopped traffic on the street and he was known for the next few days as "pom-pom."

In Stewart the only article of native interest for sale is beaded belts. These cost three dollars and say ALASKA on them. One day after we have arrived, all of them are gone from the store.

In Vancouver, our uniforms came from Three Vets, the city's great army surplus store. Much of the actual cold-weather gear needed in the 40-below weather of Churchill was supplied by them, so the cast spent a lot of time there getting fitted out for the shoot.

One day Jim Tolkan, who plays one of the scientists, came back from his fitting wearing a Canadian Postal Service surplus leather jacket: "Seventy bucks to the public, they gave it to me for fifty..." By the end of the week, most of the company had their Canadian Postal Service jackets.

Jim Tolkan doesn't induce you to look on the bright side, he *is* the bright side. He is the King of Hanging Out. His room in Vancouver was stuffed with souvenirs: fur-lined World War I flight goggles, old but mint-condition riding boots, handmade knives he found in an obscure corner of Vancouver. He is a fashion plate and could make a gunnysack look elegant. He is always having a good time. Everyone wants to wear what he is wearing. He is an actor of much experience on the road, and he turns every stop into a happy treasure hunt. He is, unfortunately, not with us in Stewart/Hyder.

At night in Hyder, one could lounge about the bar of the Sealaska Hotel shooting pool or playing video games ("Good to be back in the States") or go down to the Border pub and get Hyderized.

Hyderization is the consumption of a straight shot of a local white alcohol called Moon, which is about three billion proof. One stands between two metal handrails of the bar service station. The rails are twisted and gnarled—presumably by the gyrations of those communicants who have gone before. One is given, free, a shot glass of the aforesaid liquor and must down it in one gulp. Should it refuse to stay down or the drinker refuse to stay up, he or she must buy a round for the house.

One member of the cast was only seen evenings during our three weeks in Stewart. He was on call to shoot a standby scene. And it was evident that we had so much scheduled work to do that he was never going to get called. He didn't work the whole three weeks and, depressed and Hyderized, pub-crawled through the northern nights and slept out his days in the privacy of the Edward.

MONARCHY

In Stewart, British Columbia, shooting took place on the glacier. There was a small but real danger of avalanche, and a watch was set up and evacuation procedures planned. There were not enough helicopters, of course, to take the whole crew off at once, and someone asked, in the event of an emergency, how we would evacuate the site. "We'll evacuate in order of billing," a crew member quipped, and everyone laughed. But, of course, we *would* evacuate in order of billing. The movie is built around the star, and with the ice coming down the mountain, all attention would turn unthinkingly to hustling him into the plane while droves of women and children—joining in the general anxiety for his safety—looked on. For the star of the film is not only an avatar to the audience, he is the Prince of the Movie. He stands for the movie, and so, like other princes, he stands for ourselves. One day in May, Tim Hutton was hurt by a rock falling on his foot. Work, of course, stopped while all looked on and then looked away in a hush. A thick anxiety spread over the set and rippled over to the production office, where calls were going out for ambulances, and over to the lunch truck, where people were talking in whispers. A man who didn't know what had happened came into the production office cracking a joke and was told to shut up: "Don't you know what happened?"

The Film Industry is the American Monarchy: it is strict entailed succession and Horatio Alger in one. Except for the money manipulators and speculators on the top, it is a society built on work, achievement, and fealty to those in power.

At the lower levels one's superiors have the right either to bestow or to deny employment, and at the upper levels they have the right to ennoble, to elevate out of the realm of the workaday and into the realm of power: the star's boyfriend/ girlfriend made a "producer," and so on. Also, as in any good monarchy, there is the American Element of Luck: who just *happened* to be there when the star got sick, the runaway carriage of the Daughter of a Wealthy Manufacturer saved by the Newsboy.

THE GREAT CHAIN OF BEING

Several of us are dining out on Sunday. We are in the charge of John Lone who plays the Iceman, and Michael Westmore, the makeup artist. They have formed an ad hoc supper club. They seek out the culinary hotspots of Vancouver and share their finds with the rest. But Sunday evenings in Vancouver are usually spent at the Paradise, the *in* room of a larger Chinese restaurant. John orders for us all in Chinese. The dinner is magnificent. After dinner our conversation turns to film gossip. We all chuckle at the idea that Lana Turner was actually discovered on a stool at Schwab's, but we earnestly recount to each other how we know for a fact that Sly Stallone (". . . and he *deserved* it!") was discovered tearing tickets at the Sutton Theatre in New York; or that Jessica Lange was found waiting tables at the Lion's Head pub on Sheridan Square; or that George Lucas got where he is on the basis of talent. ("Do you know how much money he makes in a *day* . . . ? I have a friend who saw a check sitting on his desk . . .")

The other part of the conversation, of course, is *trashing*: "You know who's a real _____ ?" And what both parts of this fugue add up to is Belowstairs Gossip. Though we would, at first, laugh the idea to scorn, what we are doing is "talking about our betters."

If there are those greater than ourselves in luck, if there are those lesser than ourselves in talent, if, in fact, *anyone* in the business can be fixed on a scale of luck, talent, achievement, success, then we can compare ourselves to that point on the scale and, in a quite real sense, *know our place*. We can then see that, moment to moment, life is very ordered, and that, within this structure, there is the possibility for change and advancement.

This feeling of *knowing one's place* is a good feeling, and mostly absent in our contemporary culture in which one generally compares oneself to one's peers with either vanity tinged with dread or envy tinged with dread.

At our various bull sessions, *everyone* says (with some surprise), "You know, I kind of wish we were back in the old studio days." None of us really knows what those good old days were like, but we all long for order, and dream of that imaginary society which would make us feel secure.

IDENTITY IN CRAFT

Patrick Palmer says that one can usually identify a film worker's job by his or her appearance. Each job, as one might expect, attracts a person with the emotional and physical predisposition for that job—much in the way that people choose dogs they feel best exemplify their own personal strong suits.

In the film industry (as in the theater), this phenomenon is very pronounced. The makeup woman, the costume designer, and the still photographer (that person responsible for making a still-photographic record of the appearance and the action on the set) are always *very* attractive and special looking.

(Lorey Sebastian is our still photographer. She, out of the goodness of her heart, became our social director, organizing a cinematheque in her room every night in Vancouver, sightseeing excursions, Crouse's surprise party, a Canadian Strip-O-Gram to celebrate the birthday of Don Levy, the unit publicist, etc.)

The sound recordist and the editor are usually introverted endomorphs—Dungeons and Dragons types. The producers (they seem to come in pairs) are always Mutt and Jeff: one is a smiler and one is a worrier. (On this film Jewison is the smiler.) The stuntmen are always good-looking and seem to behave in the extroverted way in which people assume that movie stars behave. The movie stars behave like wallflowers. The teamsters (the people who drive the film's cars, trucks, and station wagons) are usually potbellied, quiet, and kind.

A CANADIAN DIGRESSION

One day I was sitting in one of our station wagons outside a film supply house in Vancouver. The teamster was waiting to pick up some equipment and we had some time to kill as the man he was go get it from was at lunch. He saw a young prostitute across the street looking for trade and proceeded to speak about her in some intricate detail: her habits, her personality, her history. I remained noncommittal as I didn't know what the correct response was. Obviously something between "Everybody has to have a hobby" and "Mmmm."

Another prostitute came on the corner and the teamster began a similar rendition of *her* life story, personality, and attributes. They were joined by a third and on he went. There was a pause in the conversation; it was my turn to speak. Not wishing to appear a fool, and struck by his garrulousness (this was, after all, Canada), I said, rather tentatively, "You sure seem to know a lot about these young women." He explained that his wife ran a halfway house for them.

So my illusions about Canadians remained intact; although, curiously, the teenage hookers of Vancouver seem—to a transient—to be the most prominent cultural touchstone of this very Calvinist city. The cabdrivers point them out to you— much as in Chicago a quarter-century ago, one was driven through the ghetto as a tourist attraction. One reads about these hookers and proposed laws to deal with them in the local editorials constantly; the streets around our hotel are labyrinthine with random islands, malls, and roundabouts, and we are told this was done to cut down on the traffic of cruising johns. And on last Easter morning, many of the hookers dressed as Easter bunnies. This last impressed us all greatly as, professionally, we approve of any show of spirit: which is why we all loved the softball game.

US AND THEM

Patrick Palmer and Don Levy, our unit publicist, arranged the game with the Arts Club Theatre of Vancouver. We got to the park early and started warming up, and Patrick showed up with his clipboard, took notes on our performance, and assigned positions and batting order.

Jim VanWyck, first assistant director, played AAA ball with the Minnesota Twins farm team. *He* could have been the captain, but it was certainly more fun to see Patrick in his sweatsuit scribbling in his clipboard.

Palmer is a taciturn and somewhat forbidding man. Many thought he was a stick-in-the-mud and labeled him standoffish until it was discovered he started in the film business as a craft serviceman—that person responsible for maintenance of the coffee urns and snacks on the set, at which point his stock shot up immediately. To the most extent in films, and completely in the theater, we all enter from the bottom.

How wonderful it was to be American at that softball game. We were cheering each other on and booing the bad calls, we were giving each other high five. Tech people the actors had only nodded to on the set were doing circus catches in the outfield and getting their day in court. The day was perfect, we were sweating, we were exercising, we were killing them, the sun was shining on the mountains across the Sound, and the best of all David Strathairn—who plays Dr. Singe, one of the surgeons who bring the Iceman back to life—had brought a small grapefruit, just the size of the softball, and lovingly painted it white.

In the top of the eighth, with the score 12–5 (us), the pitcher put the grapefruit over the plate in a perfect slow strike and the Arts Club batter sunk into a powerhouse swing and blasted that grapefruit for all he was worth. The grapefruit exploded, spraying rind and juice and pulp in a halo I can still see, and the batter's mind turned to Jell-O. He started for first, he faltered, he blinked. The underpinnings of his world collapsed, and for a long three or four seconds he and the opposing team and all their fans and family, having been chastened by our athletic expertise, were reduced to awe and wonder by our thaumaturgy. It was, in short, a perfect moment. Perhaps, the pitcher said later that night, the one perfect moment of his life. All the next week, it kept cropping up in conversations at lunch: "Boy, you missed it. You missed the *grapefruit....*"

XENOPHOBIA

The softball game marked, more or less, the end of the shoot. Filming continued for three more weeks but everyone felt that the back of the long project had been broken.

People started talking about future plans, movies coming up, vacations, getting back to the comfort of *The New York Times*. We began trading stories about the unpleasantness of Canadians.

One crew member was asked to extinguish his cigar in a Vancouver poolroom as it offended the patrons; an actor was told to remove his baseball hat in the hotel racquetball club as it was in violation of the dress code. These incidents are discussed and rehashed for days. We all agree that the Canadian accent seems to be getting worse.

Now, the Canadians of Vancouver are, for good and ill, a placid people. There is little or nothing offensive in them. We are projecting our xenophobia onto *them. We* want to go home. We feel the job is finished and we want to go home. We have spent four months away from our loved ones and possessions in 50-below weather, beyond the Last Black Post (as Fred and Ian would have it, or, alternative, "in the wuup-

wuup"). We have been eating hotel food for months in a city where people slavishly obey the traffic laws, and enough is enough.

(It seems to me that actors—quick to grasp and easy to worry—have about two speeds when it comes to talking about work: (1) "I'm never going to work again," and (2) "I'm going to be stuck in this lousy play, soap opera, movie *forever. . . .*")

PRIDE

In any case, the day before the softball game, we are shown the rough cut of the first half hour of the film. The company works six days a week, twelve to sixteen hours a day. Saturday night, the twelfth of May, Fred Schepisi, the director, announces that after dailies (the viewing of the previous day's developed footage) he will be showing a rough cut of the first half hour of the picture—that is, a rough-edited, trial assemblage of the film's first half hour.

The company is amazed and impressed. Most directors would not show a rough cut at this stage to anyone who did not have the contractual right to see it. It is always dangerous to show half-finished work to a child, as the proverb has it, and one never knows how wagging tongues might misinterpret (or *correctly* interpret) a rough-finished product. Many directors won't even let the actors see dailies. So the company as a whole and the actors especially take Fred's gesture of showing the rough cut as a great compliment: he is, incontrovertibly, acknowledging *everyone* as having a share in the making of the movie.

So at the end of a ninety-hour workweek, we sit in part of a warehouse on the second floor of a building at Dominion Bridge (where much of the Golden Gate was built), sipping beers, waiting to see the rough cut.

First, we see the previous day's dailies. The scene shot the day before is one in which Tim Hutton, Lindsay, and the Iceman, John Lone, are in the Vivarium, a huge terrarium built to simulate tropical conditions in which the Neanderthal lived 20,000 years ago.

The Iceman, whom Tim, the anthropologist, has befriended, and with whom he learns to communicate, develops a passion for Lindsay, the doctor, and makes advances toward her. Tim intervenes and the Iceman concludes that she is Tim's woman. He then tries to barter with Tim for her and when Tim refuses, the Iceman realizes that he is all alone. He has no woman, he is in a foreign world, and he will never get home.

John Lone played the scene in a four-minute take—he is playing, basically, silently, with one or two grunts, and his acting is so pure, his intentions moment to moment completely unmistakable. Rather than playing the Iceman as a grunting gorilla, he gives his entire self to the scene, editing nothing, sparing himself nothing. We see how high the stakes are for him, and when he fails in his attempt to find companionship in an alien world, his realization is *devastating*.

After his take, there is silence and then *prolonged* loving applause. We are proud of him, we are proud to know him, and it is obvious that the movie is going to "work."

The magic of the moment is also, of course, informed by Fred's gesture of letting us *see* the rough cut; we have been permitted to apostrophize the film. It is our film, and it is a beautiful film.

The dailies continue with snippets of other scenes and, while they are going on, one by one, the principal actors go over to John and congratulate him—those who have not worked directly with him somewhat awed: "Mother of mercy, that fellow can *act....*" He is very touched and somewhat overcome.

Every one of his days has started at five A.M. with several hours of makeup. He has spent twelve to sixteen hours a day made up, head and body, he has kept himself to himself and done a magnificent job, and the warehouse room is full of the idea that that work we have just seen embodies all that is best about ourselves as People in the Theater.

All of us in the movie have reached some sort of artistic middle age. Being middle-aged we are presented with a *new* task, which is to learn to accept ourselves. We're no longer struggling against casting agents, producers, script readers, and the Artistic Establishment. We have arrived, or it is clear that the way is open to us. And what we see before us is a life of hard work, difficult living conditions, not much glamour, not much leisure. A life in which we are going to have to give ourselves those rewards we would like to enjoy.

The Theater today can provide, at best, an intermittent living. Even to the most accomplished. We may long for the days when a writer, director, or actor could live in New York and work year to year on provocative material and experience financial security. *None* of those things is possible anymore. So the theatrical worker is torn: Yes, there is a play I would like to do, but it means two months in Chicago, or Seattle, at a minimum wage and away from my family. Just so with the movies. Fewer and fewer are made every year. They are made on bizarre locations. Many times one is among strangers, working without a common history or vocabulary. Much time is devoted during and after work to establishing credentials and good faith. . . .

We have, effectively, been thrust back to the nineteenth century, to the days of touring companies and pickup casts, when the stage vehicle was built around the Star and the rest of the cast were not even given the script, but "sides," those lines which they said and the cues which preceded those lines. We are tritzing around the world eating a lot of Chinese food and spending many days saying, "But, you see, I love you. . ." or "Get the roast, oops! There's the doorbell."

And many of us experience the malaise of feeling that somehow our life got lost, that the gods have punished us by answering our prayers. We will never get back to Kansas and we will never have the doorman at the studio or the doorman at the Barrymore Theatre nod to us and ask us about our children. We feel that we are becoming a bizarre diplomatic corps, never getting home, cycled as soon as we start to Go Native, seeing old friends intermittently every half-decade or so. . . .

This is perhaps a bit melodramatic, but there you are, and that's the prejudice of *my* profession.

But Fred's invitation to see the rough cut and John Lone's work in the take have turned us around, and we're all thinking, *I* know what I'm missing, an interest in my work. That's why I got involved in this whole business in the first place, I loved the work." The projectionist brings up the lights and starts changing the reels. Fred makes the speech every director (stage or screen) makes when showing something other than the absolutely finished product: "What you are going to see is *rough*, we're still working on it, it doesn't have the *music*, the *sound* isn't right, we're still working on the editing, please keep this in mind."

People run over to the card tables for some more pretzels or carrot sticks or beer, the lights come down, and we start watching the movie.

The movie is beautiful. It is lovingly shot; Ian seems to have made even the shots of the machines simple and eloquent. It is simply and gracefully edited. The whole film is pervaded by a sense of loss: the blue-green colors of the huge ice block in which the Neanderthal is found. Rondy Johnson's costumes that transform the ordinary work clothes of the scientists; she has made the clothes, and so helped make the people, very personal.

We are watching a film about real people. They are doing their job, they are isolated in the Far North, forced to rely on each other. We are watching a film about ourselves.

We *are* those people. We *were* those people in the Far North, forced to rely on each other. And those quirks and idiosyncrasies we see on the screen are not the weak formulations of actors trying to "create a character," but, rather, the unknown and loved idiosyncrasies of people whom we know, and we are watching them doing their job. We are seeing the true revelation of character: how people react under pressure.

And as in any piece of art, the theme seems to have magically asserted itself in all aspects of the work: it is a film about a good man who isn't ever going to get home, and *we* are that good man.

Everybody is high on the film after the first half hour; then, abruptly, the rough cut ends. We are as upset as if the projector broke, but there is nothing more to see. That's as much as Billy and Fred have done. We want to see more. No one is unaware that this feeling and its expression are a traditional and expected compliment after seeing a rough cut, but, nevertheless, we are surprised and pleased to feel it.

Fred and Ian Baker are warmly congratulated by all. The whole company is standing around smiling at one another. "Ladies and gentlemen," says Fred, "let's get Adrian."

We go off to restaurants or bars or hotel rooms telling each other how brilliant John Lone is, Fred is, Billy is, Lindsay and Tim are, what a genius Ian is... telling each other how proud we are of ourselves as a group. And the next day is the softball game, and our pride is augmented by our trouncing of the Arts Club Theatre.

The final three weeks of filming are downhill.

It is over, Jim Tolkan is gone, Richard Monette finishes shooting a day early and shaves his beard. He is going to the Stratford Festival, where he will play seven classical leads. Patrick Palmer runs into him at lunch and asks where the beard is. Monette explains they finished his shot early and he is done with the film. "We're paying you until tomorrow," says Palmer, "put it back." Rondy Johnson, our costume designer, is retired, upset because several of the extra costumes for the last sequence have not yet been chosen. She has been let go, as money is getting very tight. The film is

running close to the wire. A sign goes up at the lunch trailer:
THE BREAKFAST BURRITOS ARE NOT FREE. IF YOU ARE NOT PRIN-
CIPAL CAST OR PRODUCTION STAFF, YOUR CHARGE IS $2.50. Horst
Grandt, the propmaster, complains that his chewing gum has
been eliminated from the craft service tables. Many people
comment, "Well, King, I guess this case is *closed.*"

A second softball game is scheduled. We are to play a
Vancouver radio station. They have a regular team, they have
their own uniforms, and they practice once a week. But our
game is scheduled over the long weekend. It is Victoria Day
in Canada and most of the station's team is on vacation out
of town, so we are pitted against their B team, and we romp
over them.

David Strathairn has brought another grapefruit, but, of
course, it is not the same.